"I have known and ministered with Dr. Flo Ellers for over thirty years. She is not only a tremendous teacher and inspiration to the church; she is that and more to me. Her friendship is as precious to me as the revelation from God's Word that she brings to my life and everyone she touches. This new book of hers, *Chief Walkin' Tall: A New Day is Dawning for Native Americans,* reveals the vital part the First Nations Christians in America will play in these last days. This is not just a prophetic word to the Church, but Flo's testimony and life are an example of what God is getting ready to do throughout Indian Country through those who believe in Jesus the Messiah. She truly demonstrates that He is not only the "white man's God," but He is the Savior, Healer, and Deliverer of people, no matter what their color and culture. As you read this book, open your heart to see and hear what the Spirit is showing and telling us. You will be changed!"

Apostle Negiel Bigpond
Morning Star Church of All Nations
Two Rivers Native American Training Center

"This is one of the best books that I've ever read, regarding our Native American people's destiny, in God. I myself have ministered to the Native people in the area of revival, and felt that a book like this was so needed. This book brings balance to the area of Native spirituality and customs. Dr. Flo Ellers is an anointed teacher of God with great prophetic insight. She has the heart and passion of a true revivalist. As a female Native American, she has lived through much prejudice and chosen to love, forgive, and bring healing to all people. We are on the fringes of the greatest move of the Holy Spirit that the Church has ever known. God is going to use His precious Native children in a great way. It is time for all of us to lay down anything that holds us back from our eternal destiny and to be identified as the people of God."

Dr. Debbie Rich Rester
Debbie Rich Ministries

"Flo did an outstanding job in writing this book. It is informative, challenging, and prophetic. It gives hope to those who are in intercession for a Holy Ghost revival. Everybody needs to read it, and hear what the Spirit is saying to the churches."

M. George Kallappa
Senior Pastor
LaPush Assembly of God

Chief
WALKIN' TALL

A New Day is Dawning for Native Americans

Flo Ellers

Address all personal correspondence to:
Dr. Flo Ellers
World Ministries International
P. O. Box 277
Stanwood, Washington 98292
Email: floellers153@gmail.com

Individuals and church groups may order books from Dr. Flo Ellers directly, or from the publisher. Retailers and wholesalers should order from our distributors. Refer to the Deeper Revelation Books website for distribution information, as well as an online catalog of all our books.

Published by
Deeper Revelation Books
Revealing "the deep things of God" (1 Cor. 2:10)
P.O. Box 4260
Cleveland, TN 37320
Phone: 423-478-2843
Email: info@deeperrevelationbooks.org
Website: www.deeperrevelationbooks.org

Deeper Revelation Books assists Christian authors in publishing and distributing their books. Final responsibility for design, content, permissions, editorial accuracy, and doctrinal views, either expressed or implied, belongs to the author.

DEDICATION

This book is lovingly dedicated to my precious
family for whom it was written.

Michelle, Yvonne, Nicole and Valentina, our four
daughters and our eleven grandchildren

Jared, Stefanie, Corey, Daniel, Anthony, Rhonica,
Michael, Benjamin, Nicolas, Carmen, and Madeline.

To our kind and loving family friend,
"Nurse Kathie"

who gave wise insight to the contents and format
of this book.

Thank you so much Kathie.

ACKNOWLEDGMENTS

I am most grateful to Dr. Jonathan Hansen of World Ministries International for taking the time from his busy ministry schedule to read and write the Foreword to this book. He is a fourth generation ordained minister and currently serves on the board of the International Coalition of Apostolic Leaders. Since 1989, Dr. Hansen has been given dreams and visions from the Lord to warn the church of her condition with a message of love and repentance to prepare for the Second Coming of the Lord...which draweth nigh! He has traveled to many nations speaking prophetically from the Lord into the lives of key political and church leaders changing the course and destiny of their nation.

Deep appreciation goes to Dr. Debbie Rich who graduated from Rhema Bible Training Center and served at Rhema for a short time. In 1990, Dr. Rich moved to Alaska and revival broke out under her evangelistic prison ministry. She carried the fires of revival to the bush areas of Alaska and then to thirty-five nations of the world. She and her husband Bob Rester have recently pioneered a new work in Aberdeen, Washington, called FaithLife Church Northwest.

I want to also give thanks to my longtime friend, Rev. George M. Kallappa. He and his wife Rita hold a very special place in my heart. George was the first pastor to ask me to preach at his church when I graduated from Bible school in 1982. He has served as director of the Northwest American Indian Fellowship and he and his wife are currently serving the body of Christ as pastors of La Push Assembly of God.

I greatly appreciate and honor Dr. Negiel Bigpond for his work in the Lord and for his treasured friendship. He and his wife Jan have served the Lord faithfully in their ministry for the past thirty years as they have traveled and evangelized over 100 Native American reservations. Dr. Bigpond is a certified drug and alcohol abuse counselor. He is the apostolic leader of Morning Star Church of All Nations in Oklahoma.

SPECIAL THANKS

I want to thank my Lord and only Savior—Jesus, the Christ for His great salvation and deliverance, without which I would be eternally separated from Him.

I want to thank Him for healing my hurts and never giving up on me when others had.

I want to thank Him for teaching me how to love and forgive like Him; and to face my failures honestly so He could bring me into His great victory which comes through the Cross alone. Hallelujah!

CONTENTS

FOREWORD

I highly recommend people not only in The United States of America to read this book, *Chief Walkin' Tall*, but also people throughout the world regardless of their nation or ethnic heritage. Flo Ellers, as a Native American, identifies mental, emotional, physical, and spiritual problems not only facing and attacking her race but many of these problems and issues also affect every race and people groups across humanity.

Definitely she identifies the difficult challenges and circumstances that Indians in America have had to endure and live through, but she also offers solutions for their dilemma. For the people who were born into good Christian homes, this book reveals and explains many of the dangers that they haven't experienced because of being protected and sheltered and hopefully, they will be wise and choose to avoid experimenting with drugs, alcohol, tattoos, and other bodily mutilations that come from the dark side of every culture and society originating from the devil who hates all people, especially women.

For all people, this book offers a glimpse and understanding of Native Americans and all people groups who have been victimized and what they have to cope with because of the exploitation of others. Flo explains how her tribe were animists and how their spiritual leader a Shaman exerted great powers to influence the weather, cure diseases, protect her people against different types of enemies, including witchcraft, even though both Shamans and witches obtained their powers from the devil. Flo also explains how some people in her tribe had the demoniac power to change themselves from human to an animal or bird or insect which is called, *"shape shifting."* I will reiterate that this and many other truths found in this book are found throughout the world in people groups that get their power from hell itself.

This book goes into the traditions of her tribe and many other tribes and people groups that dabble in the demoniac side of reality because they do not know or have rejected the Author of truth. Animal sacrifices and people sacrifices are all involved in Native American history with the explanations of their origins and the answer and cures for the mental, physical, emotional, and spiritual destruction that it has been done to the soul of these precious people. This book is truly educational, historical, and inspirational as it gives a clear understanding how people have found themselves in the depths of despair yet have turned their lives around to have a glorious and prosperous future.

—Rev. Dr. Jonathan Hansen

Founder and President of World Ministries
International

INTRODUCTION

Several years ago, my good friend Dr. Shelli J. Manuel had a vision of the Native American. She said in the vision it was a very dark, cold winter's night with hardened snow on the ground. The sky was clear and the bright stars were twinkling down upon the earth and upon a hunter with a bow and arrows. With his alert deep-set eyes, apparently he was looking for *something* as he was cutting diagonally across the United States. There was an eerie silence except for the slight sound of his moccasins as they lightly touched the glistening snow covered ground. Suddenly, he must have heard a noise because he stopped and cautiously looked to the right, and then to the left. He did not see what had made the sound, so he slowly lifted his head upward looking to the heavens and whispered, "I can feel Your Presence, but I don't know Your Name."

God's Plan for the Native Americans

Twenty years ago, the Spirit of the Lord changed my name to *Wind that Fans the Flame.* This happened prophetically because I was about to step into a new move of God—a revival of signs, wonders, and miracles in many places around the world. I was not *the* wind that would bring the revival—no, a thousand times no—but only a vessel to usher in *The Wind of God* who is the Great Holy Spirit. If you are interested, you can read the account of a few of these revival meetings in my books *Activating the Angelic,* and another I coauthored titled *Threshold of Glory.*

In the Bible when God was about to change the destiny of a man or woman to affect a nation, He would change his or her name. He changed the name Abram, which means "exalted father," to Abraham, which means "Father of a multitude." He changed the name *Saul,* meaning, "asked for" to *Paul,* a Roman name meaning "little" or "humble." It was a name befitting this early church leader because he considered himself the least of all the apostles. However, that happened a very long time ago. Nevertheless, God is still working in the hearts of men and women, changing them and changing nations through them.

In *Chief Walkin' Tall,* I will continue the saga of a forgotten people—the Native Americans—forgotten by man, but not by God. A heavenly fire is falling on tribes throughout North America purging out the dross and sanctifying them unto Himself. The wind of the Holy Spirit is blowing away the chaff that they may step into their destiny as end time visionaries and revivalists to help usher in a move of God with signs following.

One particular indigenous tribe of the Native Americans lives on the coastal lands of Southeast Alaska. They are the *Tlingit,* which means "The People," or "The People of the Tides." I belong to this tribe. Today, many young Tlingit are looking back to their tribal religion for a sense of identity

18

and purpose. Yet another group is trying to reconcile Christianity with their traditional culture. In addition to these groups, many of the elders have converted to a belief in God's Son, the One they call in our language *Dee Kee on Kow do Yeet*. Dissentions arise out of misunderstanding, but the great Holy Spirit from above will help the members of each group to find their identity in Him and bring peace to their souls.

When Paul the apostle stood on Mars Hill to address the Greeks, he knew it was a capital offense to preach a new deity in Athens, so he used the inscription TO THE UNKNOWN GOD, a deity they already acknowledged, to present the Gospel to them. God's wisdom flowed through him as he made the following appeal: Then Paul stood in the midst of the Areopagus and said, "Men of Athens, I perceive that in all things you are very religious, for as I was passing through and considering the objects of your worship, I even found an altar with this inscription:

TO THE UNKNOWN GOD

Therefore, the One whom you worship without knowing Him I proclaim to you: God, who made the world and everything in it, since He is Lord of heaven and earth, does not dwell in temples made with hands. Nor is He worshipped with men's hands, as though He needed anything, since He gives to all life, breath, and all things. And He has made from one blood every nation of men to dwell on all the face of the earth, and has determined their pre-appointed times and the boundaries

> *of their dwellings, so that they should seek*
> *the Lord, in the hope that they might grope*
> *for Him and find Him, though He is not far*
> *from each one of us; for in Him we live and*
> *move and have our being, as some of your own*
> *poets have said, 'For we are also His offspring.'*
> *Therefore, since we are the offspring of God,*
> *we ought not to think that the Divine Nature*
> *is like gold or silver or stone, something shaped*
> *by art and man's devising (Acts 17:22-29).*

While the Native Americans are seeking solace and
their destiny, the Creator is reaching out in love to
tell us, "You are not just *a* people, but that you can
become *the* people of God." His Word declares to
those who have already accepted Him as their Savior-
Chief:

> *But you are a chosen generation, a royal*
> *priesthood, a holy nation, His own special*
> *people, that you may proclaim the praises of*
> *Him who called you out of darkness into His*
> *marvelous light; who once were not a people but*
> *are now the people of God. . . . (1 Peter 2:9-10).*

Chief Walkin' Tall is my story and yet it is *our*
story. It is about our lives, discarded and rejected
by man—lives so broken and unwanted, the will
to stand up was gone until Jesus came and picked
us up. He whispers in our heart, "Stand tall my
warrior-daughter, stand upright my warrior-son,
for you are no longer an outcast; you are my *Chief
Walkin' Tall."*

_Klawock, Alaska, Prince of Wales Island, off the coast of SE
Alaska. This is the village where I was born and raised and
where the revival of signs and wonders broke out in 1954._

Hole-in-the-Wall, Alaska, our summer fishing camp

Pastors Walter and Harriet Williams
of Kake, Alaska

_My sister
Charlotte & Me_

_My father Norman Gannon,
½ Cherokee, from Jackson,
Mississippi_

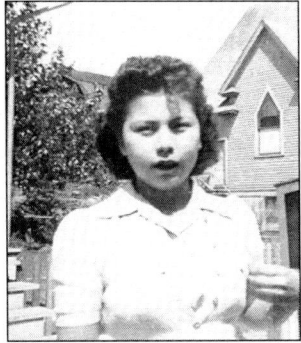

_My mother Cleo, sixteen
years old, full-blooded
Tlingit_

_Left to right…my mother Cleo Booth, and Pastors
George and Rita Kallappa, taken when they were
pastoring in Metlakatla, Alaska._

Chapter 1

THE CEREMONIAL HOUSE

My Tlingit name is *Khou-Ton* from Klawock, *Henyaa*, a small Native American village on the Prince of Wales Island off the coast of Southeast Alaska. My uncle, who was the chief of our village, gave me a second name, *Khoo-day*. That name belonged to a prophet who lived in our village in the early 1900s.

Our ancient civilization was a matrilineal society where our ancestry and inheritance passed down through our mother's line. Our clothing was tanned skins and cedar bark. We almost never wore shoes even in the wintertime. We were hardened and our skin thickened through daily bathing in the sea; therefore, we seldom succumbed to sickness. Our artistic skills produced outstanding woodcarvings with good design in bright colors of red, black, and blue.

25

Our governing authority was chiefs. Many of our chiefs practiced polygamy. The more wives and slaves a chief had, the more wealth he possessed. The slaves were war captives or purchased from neighboring tribes. Because they were an expensive possession, the chiefs treated them well. At feasts, some slaves received freedom and obtained all the rights of a freeborn Tlingit.

Historical records tell us we had our first contact with the Europeans in 1741. Then the Russians came to our land, whom we feared and hated, and later the Spanish. When the Europeans first observed us, they said we were "the most gifted of all the coastal people from Bering Strait to California." One encyclopedia had a different view of us. They said we were one of the fiercest tribes in the Pacific Northwest.

Another European perspective described us as "earnest, gloomy, austere looking," but they did not view us in our ceremonial house when we were having a feast. During a celebration, some of our elders, who had great oratory skills, never missed their opportunity to give a speech. If the speech was with humor, we found another occasion to laugh. If his or her words were with deep wisdom, we applauded with respect.

Our songs had good rhythm as we sang and danced to the beat of our drums. We loved to sit around the fire telling stories and jokes, laughing until the early hours of the morning. Time did not press us for we scarcely thought about the future but lived entirely in the moment. We were a people of the seasons.

We did not have loud outbursts of joy or sorrow, but with tender love, our mothers cared for their children. Seldom did they speak to them in a harsh tone or beat them as a form of discipline. Our society had respect for women in general and bestowed honor upon the older women known for their wisdom. Infidelity was rare, so the divorce rate was low.

When our people of the same clan would meet each other, they would affectionately say *"Ach-kani"* (my compatriot or my friend) and embrace. We were never in a hurry, so there was always time for another short story, a good laugh, or just small talk about the weather.

Many of our strong Tlingit men would undertake long canoe voyages to fish, hunt, and trade with the Europeans and our neighboring tribes of the Haida Indians and the Tsimpshian of British Columbia. Knowledge of survival skills from the fathers and uncles were passed on down to each succeeding generation of hunter-warriors.

When a young boy was growing into manhood, the parents, especially the maternal uncle, would undertake his education to train him. When the children grew into adulthood, they had learned and developed good social skills, modesty, marital faithfulness, and the giving of honor to our elders. These traits were huge among our people and still are today.

The Devil's Mutilations

However, there is a dark side in *every* culture and our society, though fairly advanced, was no exception. We had beautiful traditions, but we also had strange customs that were hurtful to our people. When the Europeans came, they documented how both sexes had tattoos and other bodily mutilations. One such disfiguring practice was the lip plug in the lower lip of the women. When a girl was about eleven or twelve years of age (sometimes even younger), they would pierce her lip and insert a piece of copper wire to keep it from growing back together. When the lip sufficiently stretched to fit the plug, they would place another larger plug that continued to stretch the lip until it became grotesque to look at. If she was the wife of a chieftain, her lip plug could be as large as a small saucer, and she would have to remove it to eat her meals.

At the end of the last century, our society would never have tolerated such horrendous abuse, but since the beginning of the 21st century, there has been a worldwide acceleration and a resurgence of the devil's mutilations deceiving humanity into thinking these abominable practices are desirable and even beautiful.

The devil hates all people made in God's image, and he particularly hates women, so he mars their beauty with lip plugs, tattoos, and other disfiguring mutilations. In some African tribes, female circumcision is practiced. Today, in many places around the world, women must suffer quietly for fear of reprisal, severe beatings, or even death. In the Middle East in 120-degree heat, men force women to cover

28

their face and body in black garb while they wear white linen clothing to ward off the extreme heat. In the Bible, and everywhere Christianity is proclaimed and established, man is freed, especially the women.

Death, War, and Transmigration of Souls

My grandmother told me in the old days when a chief had erected a new building, he would have a hole dug in the front of the ceremonial house for the heraldic column or totem pole. Then he would put one of his slaves in the hole and drop the totem on top of him, spilling his blood. During these ceremonial occasions, the Tlingit would paint his face red, as they do for hunting and war.

Native Americans have a strong sense of property rights, and any infringement on his territory is a call for war. Preparations for an attack were usually kept secret, even from the women of the tribe. Some warriors practiced flagellation to make them strong for war. My Uncle Theodore told me when a warrior went into battle, he took his implement of war, and bound it with rawhide to his hand and wrist so he would never lose his weapon in a battle. For surprise, the attacks took place under the cover of darkness, and the warriors exacted horrible cruelty toward their enemy.

My people believed in transmigration of souls. The soul of a deceased person is supposed to return to earth, and, through a pregnant woman, find its clan again. If a pregnant woman sees a dead relative in a dream, she believes that his soul had entered her. If her newborn child has any birthmark that might identify him with the dead relative, it is assumed that this person returned to the earth, so the child is given the same name. Therefore, some Tlingit who were dissatisfied with their life may want to die so that they can start over again under conditions that are more favorable by being born into the clan of some envied chief.

The belief in a life after death was widespread. Those who believed the spirit of man or his "ghost" gone to the other side of life did not have much food and water, never failed to remember the dead during a feast meal by calling out their name and throwing a little food into the fire. My friend from a southeastern Alaskan village told me she was at a potlatch and saw a Native throw some food into the fire, and the fire flamed up as if gunpowder was throw into the flames. She said she became frightened and left the gathering.

When a powerful and wealthy chief died, his body was cremated and his ashes were put in a box and attached to a pole or his attendants would put it in an elevated grave house. If he had many slaves while on earth, some of his choice slaves' hands and feet were bound and thrown into the fire with him so they could serve him in the next world. The natives preferred cremation because they believed they would find the other life warm and light, and they could always go to the fire to stay warm.

The Rattle, the Witch, and the Shaman

There was always a battle between the Shaman and the witches even though both obtained their powers from the devil. If someone in the village became

30

deathly ill, usually a named witch was the culprit. Like the Shaman, the witch possessed great power and used her skills to kill and destroy. The witch has many methods of killing a person. What I am about to tell you is only one method. Typically, when she was hired for murder, she would take a piece of clothing, or some of their hair or something else from the person she was to destroy and put that personal belonging on a dead body or something similar. As the corpse or the item began to rot, the living person slowly started to die. If the Shaman discovered what the witch had done in secret, he usually tortured and killed her.

When I was a little girl, I overheard my elders talking in our Tlingit language about a group of coastguardsmen from Ketchikan who witnessed a witch flying through the night sky. Even though we were forced to give up speaking our Tlingit language in the white government school, I could still understand what they said in Tlingit about the flying witch. When my grandmother had company and they started telling her something they did not want me to hear, she would speak to them in Tlingit saying, "She understands what you are talking about."

When I was about six or seven years old, my grandmother told me there was a witch on our island. One day, this witch from a certain village came to me trying to persuade me to go with her. I can still hear her false teeth clacking and see the spittle on her mouth as she squinted at me with her evil eyes beckoning me. If my grandma had not warned me about her, I do not know what would have happened to me that day.

The Witch's Teeth Fall Out

Several years ago when my apostolic father, Brother Victor, was still alive, he told me the following story of an incident that happened in his African country. He said he was in a remote village preaching the Gospel to the villagers. Strategically placed speakers at the front corners of the gathering funneled the sound waves into the next village a few miles away. While he was preaching the Gospel, these words flowed unintentionally out of him as the Holy Spirit spoke through him: "There is a witch at the sound of my voice, and you have been cursing this meeting and the Lord says to you, 'If you do not stop cursing this meeting, all your teeth will fall out!'" He was astounded at his own words but quickly went back to his preaching. Then he gave an altar call for salvation and many responded to the Holy Spirit's prompting.

While he was praying for those at the altar area, suddenly, a woman came screaming into the meeting and ran through the crowd to where my minister friend was. Blood was gurgling out of her mouth. When she fell on the ground before him, he cast the demon out of her and led her in a salvation prayer. She got up and stood before him toothless but gloriously saved! She explained to him that she was the witch who was cursing the meeting. My spiritual apostolic father said he saw her again many years later but before he could finish his story, I excitedly asked him, "Did her teeth grow back?" He said with a slight smile, "No, she is still toothless, but she is also still serving the Lord Jesus."

Shape Shifting

When I visited a missionary friend of mine who lived in Oregon, she told me a short story about an incarcerated native man from one of the northern reservations. She said that one day when the jailer had gone to look in on him, he was gone. He had simply vanished! Another friend of mine, who is a prophet/pastor, shared with me another frightening story about a Christian woman who lives on one of the reservations in Washington State. One night, she heard someone walk into her house. When she saw who it was, she stared at him and then slowly looked down at his feet, which were animal hoofs! He was a centaur. He looked at her, spit on the floor, and left. The spittle left a terrible odor. She attempted to clean it up, but the foul smell remained. A minister came to her home and anointed the floor with oil, and the odor left.

When a person has the ability, aided by demon power, to change from a human to an animal, an insect, or a bird, they call that *shape shifting*. It still happens today not only on the Native American reservations or First Nations reserves but also in the dark corners of the earth. For instance, in shape shifting, they can change from a man to a deer and back to a man again and many other forms. Even today, captives of Satan, master of the underworld, practice these wicked acts. The Bible says Satan (or the devil) comes to steal, kill, and destroy us, but only Jesus, God's Son, is here to give us an abundant, overflowing life! (See John 10:10). Hallelujah!

Chapter 2

THE "UNCIVILIZED TRIBES" OF ALASKA

The Europeans first introduced my people, the Tlingit to alcohol. It became a horrible plague of the devil to destroy us. At first, we refused the brandy, whiskey, and vodka because we were afraid of losing control and falling into the hands of the Russians. We gradually fell captive to the drink. However, we became hostile, committing crimes as our violent passions ignited. Then we became addicted to alcohol, and if we did not have the money or goods for trade to buy the drink, we sold our wives and daughters to the men on the ships anchored in our harbor.

As a natural consequence of prostitution, our family members contracted syphilis and other sexually transmitted diseases. The whites continued to come to our shores bringing the "fire water" to our people. However, not all of the whites were bad. A few of the American officials were very good men

35

who tried to stop all the destructive customs and the drunkenness. They were successful to a degree; but not until the Gospel of Jesus Christ came, were the captives set free.

The Three Apostles

In 1793, Empress Catherine II, at the request of Baranof and Shelikof, issued an official decree that priests should be sent to the new Alaskan colonies to spread Christianity among the heathen. The ship called *The Three Apostles* brought seven monks, among them Joasaf, an Augustinian, through whose efforts in 1796 built the first Christian church on Kodiak Island.

In 1857, William Duncan from Highbury College in London, England was sent by a missionary society to start a work among the First Nations people of Canada in Fort Simpson, British Columbia (BC). Eventually, they moved the Tsimshian Indians of British Columbia to the only reserve in Alaska, a place called Metlakatla. Under his efforts, Metlakatla became a *model village* on the coast. He taught the Tsimshian many skills until they greatly excelled in business, music, government, and industry. (Some details of the account of the Tlingit and Tsimshian were obtained from *The Tlingit Indians* by Aurel Krause, Translated by Erna Gunther. The original edition of this work was published in 1885.)

My village of Klawock also received the Gospel with signs, wonders, and miracles under the ministry of Missionary/Evangelists Leroy and Grace Henysel of Montana. To read a partial report of this glorious outpouring, go to my book, *Wind That Fans the Flame!*

The Blood of a Martyr

In the summer of 1992, a Tlingit pastor named Walter Williams of Kake, Alaska, invited me along with a large team of ministers such as Pastors Negiel Bigpond, Sheila Marks, and Les Moore from the "Lower 48" to hold a camp meeting at his church. After the successful meetings concluded, Pastor Williams gave me a small booklet about a very intriguing story. It concerned two men and a woman who changed the destiny of their village of Kake and brought the people out of bondage. Here is a small portion of their story.

> *William Henry Seward purchased Alaska from Czarist Russia for the United States for a little over $7 million. Article 3 of the treaty of cession, which was ratified by the U.S. on May 28, 1867, stated the following with regard to the people living in the ceded territory: "If they should prefer to remain . . . they, with the exception of the uncivilized tribes, shall be admitted to the enjoyment of all the rights and immunities of citizens of the United States."*

The Tlingit was one of the "uncivilized tribes" who had no "enjoyment of all the rights and immunities" as a citizen of the U.S. Yet, this was our land! When Seward purchased Alaska, he not only purchased our vast land, he also bought human lives as well.

During those years after the purchase of Alaska, God sent a peaceful Quaker, the Reverend Charles Edwards, who first took the Good News to Kake, and died there, before he saw his harvest. Under Reverend Edwards's ministry, a few Tlingit converted to Christianity, but he had a great task before him as he attempted to help them let go of some of their dark customs. One day, a schooner laden with liquor put into Kake's waters to sell alcohol and other goods to the Tlingit. Reverend Edwards, fearing the effect of the liquor on his little group of converts, went from house to house in the village warning them not to touch the fiery destruction the trader had brought. The vessel moved into the tideway, but by night, small boats carried the dangerous and destructive cargo ashore.

He then faced the schooner's captain, who, in a rage of protest, brutally shot down the gentle Quaker on the deck of the liquor-trading schooner. Mortally wounded, Reverend Edwards was thrown onto the beach where he died. Standing close by, a young Tlingit Chief named Charles Newton grieved over his newfound pastor-friend's death. He learned early in life what it means to lay down one's life for the sheep.

The Healer-Chief

Some of the exasperated villagers hated the white men who continually came into the sea-lanes given to them by their fathers, so they brutally attacked the whites. The U.S. Government retaliated and sent in a gunboat and blew up the town! Kake's gunboat incident and a thousand similar stories attribute to the anger, hatred, and brooding sadness in the eyes of the Native Americans. However, Kake was not left in its shattered, resentful misery. Heaven was preparing a "Healer-Chief." The young, kind chief,

Charles Newton, had been ordained in the Salvation Army as a sergeant. Wanting to help his parents with the Gospel effort in his village, he went to Chemawa Indian School at Salem, Oregon. When asked there why he sought to study, he replied, "My father cannot read or write. He has given his heart to God and is leading The Salvation Army in Kake. I have come to learn how to read and write so that I can be his hands and eyes in that work."

Two years after his schooling, Charles returned to his village and married Belle who worked tirelessly by his side as a schoolteacher and Salvationist. One day, Belle became gravely ill and was taken to a hospital in Petersburg, Alaska. Two hours before she died, she crawled out of her bed and knelt to pray by name for every unsaved person in Kake!

Before Belle went home to Glory, she inspired and encouraged her husband Charles in his long fight for the Kake people to be recognized as full-fledged citizens of the United States, with voting rights and self-government for their community. Chief Charles and Belle had a minister-friend named Reverend George Beck of the Presbyterian Church. Reverend Beck realized that the Tlingit were the only tribe that did not have reservation protection. He stated his fears that if they were not able to secure such recognition immediately, they would lose their land and the possibility of future protection.

Charles and Belle saw the danger and began to crusade. Chief Charles went to Juneau, the government seat for Alaska. There he received his own papers as

39

an American citizen, thus ending for himself the classification of membership in the "uncivilized tribes" mentioned in Seward's treaty of cession with Russia. He returned to begin the difficult task of convincing the people of Kake that they should seek the same recognition. This meant a complete renunciation of the evil customs as Indian people.

The Silver Spike

Months of tactful persuasion preceded the day when the people of Kake finally decided to ask to become American citizens. Charles offered the use of his boat for the journey to Wrangell, where the necessary formalities could take place, but Chief Charles was told the matter must be referred to Washington, D.C. Long months of correspondence ensued. Finally, victory came for the people of Kake! Charles took his boat a second time to Wrangell, and on January 6, 1912, the village of Kake was recognized formally as the abode of law-abiding American citizens. Their first mayor was appointed, along with a town council of twelve men. Charles Gunnuck, the first mayor, made his inaugural speech, a landmark in Tlingit history:

> *"Our fathers in previous years have taught us their beliefs in our superstitions, witchcrafts, burying of our dead, and erection of our totems.*
>
> *"In accepting this new way of living, everything will be contrary to what we have been taught. Needless to say, it will not be an easy task and will require a great deal of self-discipline and what we have been taught in the Christian religion as faith in God.*

> *"I have here in my hand a spike made of solid silver. Silver is valuable, and this represents the value we have placed on our early training and customs. It is as though we were to place in a box our witchcraft, superstitions, and other dark things. That box is to be nailed shut with this spike, signifying our complete change of beliefs.*
>
> *"I can think of no better person to drive this spike than Mrs. Charles Newton, whose example of courage symbolizes the courage we will need to keep our resolution. Her progressive nature represents the progress we hope to make as years go by; [and] her purity represents our new Christian religion which teaches us purity of mind and soul, without which we shall fail."*

Belle Newton drove the silver spike into the sidewalk with her customary vigor, and every year since, "Kake Day" is observed and celebrated with festivities.

Chapter 3

A Very Determined Tlingit Child

Sockeye, chum, and king salmon were so abundant around our island that in 1878, a San Franciscan firm came and built the first fish cannery in Alaska in our village of Klawock. By 1947, it was in full production and the Chinese, Japanese, and Filipino joined our villagers, working twelve hours a day.

My mother was among the young and strong workers who toiled the long hours until dark. The only break the workers had was to eat lunch and dinner the Filipino cooked at the mess hall. They were the best cooks and always ended their meals with a sheet cake smothered in butter frosting. My mom rarely ate all her dessert but brought the larger portion home for my sister and me to enjoy. She would keep it in her room, along with a large oblong box of vanilla ice cream cones. On the weekend, she would go to Bob's store, buy some ice cream, and with a big scoop, dig out the ice cream, push it into the cones, and give it to us. The ice cream would melt in our mouths and run down the corners of our chins, but we would not waste one bit of this delectable dessert. We licked our lips until we consumed all of it—including what ran down our faces.

One day, I remembered the box of ice cream cones hidden in Mom's bedroom, and I was determined to find it. I was on a mission. Struggling to get up the stairs, I looked up and saw my mother descending. I was not about to move out of her way, so I said, "Get the h#** out of my way." When I saw the shocked look on her face, I knew I was in big trouble. Even though I was only two years old at the time, I already had this uncanny ability to know when I had stepped over the line. Just as soon as that command came out of my mouth, I nervously looked at her and gave a staccato laugh as I slowly backed down the stairs.

The Killer Whales

With summer ended and with Grandpa's pockets full of money from his summer fishing, Grandpa, Grandma, and I packed our bags and boarded Grandpa's boat, *Gracie*. We were heading to Ketchikan to buy some staple foodstuff for the winter. My mother had already flown over on Ellis Airlines to spend some of her hard-earned money after the fish cannery closed for the season.

Once we got past the quiet Klawock inlet, we headed for open water. The sea was calm and the sun was shining in my face as I stood on the deck, taking in deep breaths of salty air. I loved the smell of the sea and enjoyed watching the porpoises play in the water and the sea gulls diving for a morsel of fish or a small herring.

As Grandma was looking out over the horizon, in the distance she saw large and small fins sticking out of the water. Grandpa came out of the wheelhouse to talk to Grandma and pointed to the large pod of killer whales. After he went back to the wheelhouse to navigate the boat, Grandma watched as the fins disappeared under the water. After a few minutes elapsed, she yelled to Grandpa Isaac to come quickly out of the wheelhouse. The pod of killer whales had circled our small boat. When he saw the danger, he yelled, "Get below!"

Grandma's face was full of fear as she screamed at me, "Florence, go down below now!" I crawled onto one of the bunks and covered myself with a blanket. Every few minutes, I felt the boat roll to one side and then to the other, so I would peek out the small porthole to see if it was the killer whales rocking our boat. Finally, we saw the community of Ketchikan and felt a sigh of relief as *Gracie* moored securely to the dock.

Sugar Diabetes

We checked into the Ingersoll Hotel and my grandparents took me to our room and instructed me to stay in the room with the door locked until they returned from shopping. They were gone a long time and I was getting bored, so I opened the window to put food on the ledge so the sea gulls and pigeons would come to me and eat. One pigeon, bolder than the others, remained on the ledge, waiting for me to give him more food. I wanted to give my adopted pet bird a name, but I could not think of a good one. Then I remembered overhearing my grandparents talking in Tlingit a few days earlier about a problem. In the middle of their conversation, I heard an English word I had never heard before. I have always liked words, and these words, *sugar diabetes,* caught my attention. Not knowing what the words meant, I called out to my newly named pet pigeon, "Come here, Sugar Diabetes; come and get your food!" We stayed in Ketchikan for several days. Every time I went to the window to put food out, Sugar Diabetes was there to greet me.

Rice and Fish, the Same Old Dish

My grandparents were proud people who had a strong work ethic. Grandma would never receive welfare, but she always worked diligently to provide for her large family. However, one year the fishing season was meager and our food cache was almost empty. One day, Grandma sent me to get some dried fish from the storage room. There was only one-half dried salmon left in the bottom of the barrel. I reached down for it and almost fell in because the barrel was so deep and I was so little. I gave it to Grandma who scrapped off the mold and put it in a pot of boiling water with some potatoes from her garden. We dipped the fish and potatoes in Hooligan grease or oil and went to bed without any berries for dessert.

Our Mason-jarred huckleberries and blueberries were gone, and there was no more sugar or canned milk in the cupboard. So for the first time, Grandma was forced to accept a handout from our government. Reluctantly she went to the distribution center and picked up her share of flour, sugar, powered milk, cheddar cheese, pinto beans, and butter. The butter was placed in salted water in a barrel to keep it from getting rancid through the long winter months.

We could smell Grandma's cooking in the kitchen, and we could hardly wait to sit down and eat dinner at the long table that Grandpa built. At that time, we had eaten so much fish our mouths were salivating for the bread and beans. Throughout that school year, we would come home for our lunch break. Looking at the fried, boiled, or baked fish, we would chime in together under our breath (so Grandma could not hear us), "Rice, fish, and the same old dish." Then, thanks to the government, we got a new menu! Just as soon as our elders finished blessing the food, we slathered butter on the Indian Fry Bread and put a spoon of pinto beans with small bits of bacon fat into our hungry mouths, relishing every mouthful. It tasted so good I felt like saying the blessing all over again!

Koosh-da-Kah

One spring day Grandma told me to get ready for a visit to see her Christian friend Edna who lived at the edge of town. I am not sure why she wanted to make this rare visit, but she seemed in a hurry to see her friend. As we approached Edna's house, suddenly we heard loud animal sounds. Looking in the direction of the growling, we saw this huge black animal in an evergreen tree. It must have been at least ten feet tall, with long black hairs all over its massive, gorilla-like body. With its fists tightly clenching a large branch, and with intimidating gestures, the animal shook the branch aggressively as it growled at us. I could feel the anxiety in my grandmother's tightening grip on my hand. Abruptly she let go, looked at me, and yelled, "Run Florence! Run! Don't look back until you reach Edna's house!"

My beautiful grandmother, a short, rotund woman, scurried as fast as she could and reached Edna's house in a sweat, locking the door behind her. I think my grandma was going to Edna's house to discuss this evil creature.

From time to time, our villagers had encounters with this horrible animal who roamed our island. We called him in Tlingit, the *Koosh-da-kah*. There had been recent reports of many sightings of him around our village and telltale signs around our homes. One of the signs were dozens of overlapping footprints of the *Koosh-da-kah*, so our men took plaster of paris and made a mold of his footprints just to see how large this creature was. The cast measured approximately three times the size of a man's foot. After this discovery, our villagers did not go outdoors at night for fear of being harmed by this foul-smelling creature.

Trying to Make a Deal with God

We all boarded *Gracie* and headed for our summer fishing spot, named Hole-in-the-Wall—a small island on the high sea where my mother Cleo was born. Grandpa Isaac anchored the boat offshore, and Uncle Johnnie started making trips to the island with our supplies. Finally, we got into the skiff. Johnnie pulled the cord one more time, twisted the handle with the engine propeller sputtering in the water, and we were off riding over the slow rolling waves toward our summer camp. As we approached the sandy seashore, I bent over the boat and watched the dark waters slowly become light green. Then I could see the ocean's floor with fish swimming around the rocks and seaweed waving on the seabed.

One day, our Uncle Johnnie was giving all the kids on the island a ride in his motorized skiff, but no one called my cousin Roberta and me to join in the fun. I have always liked facing the elements and high adventure, so I was game when Roberta suggested we go for our own boat ride on the high seas! We were only about six years old, but we knew how to row a boat. We pushed off, jumped into the skiff just as we had seen our Uncle Johnnie do it and started rowing toward the scow where boats tied up and bought their groceries and fish bait.

It was thrilling to ride the rolling waves and feel the breeze in our hair. After the thrill of the joy ride faded, we decided to turn around and head back to the beach, but our boat was caught in a rip tide. Our paddling became futile against the undercurrent. Roberta started to panic as the tide pulled us further and further out to sea. When I saw her crying, I started to laugh at her, trying to get her to row in synch with me, but she would not listen. By that time, she was sobbing loudly as she frantically rowed in the opposite direction. We started going in circles to the amusement of the men on the scow. The men on their fishing boats were chuckling at us too as we drifted past them. Finally, our Uncle Johnnie looked our direction, jumped in his skiff, gunned the engine, and rushed out to rescue us. He scolded us, tied our boat to his, and with our heads hanging low, dragged us back to shore.

Walking up the trail to our house, I looked at the window and saw the anger in my grandma's face. I knew I was going to get a spanking. I whispered a long, begging prayer, trying to make a quick deal with God. I told Him if he would rescue me from Grandma's wrath, I would be a good girl and never do that again. I felt slightly relieved after that prayer, but it was short-lived as I walked into the house. Grandma was standing just inside the door waiting for us with a big paddle in her hand. She grabbed us and spanked us so hard we never ventured out on that boat again . . . but it sure was a lot of fun while it lasted!

Chapter 4

INDIAN BOARDING SCHOOL

My seventh-grade teacher looked in my direction and said in a commanding voice, "Florence, stand up and pronounce the word on the board. Please tell us what it is or what it means." I did not know what the word meant and I surely did not know how to pronounce it, but I tried anyway. When I said the word, there was a loud snicker from my classmates. Blushing with shame, I looked at them and then looked at my teacher. With a sardonic look on her face, she seemed to enjoy my embarrassment. I looked long at her, and for the first time in my life, I felt hatred—deep hatred.

I had spent all my grade school years, from kindergarten through the sixth grade in Klawock, but once I turned twelve years old, entering middle school, my mother sent for me to stay with her in Sitka, Alaska. At that time, she was married to her fourth husband, Sam. He was a white man who was just like all her previous husbands—uncaring, unloving, and a heavy drinker who became violent when he was drunk.

Soon after I moved in with them, my mother and Sam went out to the bars and came home around 2 a.m. very intoxicated. I do not know why they were arguing, but all of a sudden, he struck her with such fury that she fell to the floor. He jumped on top of her and starting bashing her repeatedly in the face until he broke her dental work, split her lip, and blackened both eyes. While he was beating her, I got on the bed, leaped at his 6-feet 2-inch frame, and started hitting him. He grabbed me violently, threw me back on the bed, and left the apartment. Needless to say, life was not pleasant for me living away from my village.

"F" for Failure

Just before Labor Day, my mom had registered me in Sitka's middle school with my teacher, Mrs. R. She was a matronly, large-framed woman with a butch haircut. She was also an ex-officer in one of the armed services, and she ran her class like the military. When she humiliated me in front of the class, coupled with the constant turmoil in our home, I totally withdrew from school with a sullen demeanor. I refused to do any homework and my first report card had all F's.

The following year, my mom could not console me, so she sent me back to my village where I was happy again. My eighth-grade teacher, Mr. Demmert, who was a Tlingit, seemed to understand the complex, sensitive nature of the wounded Native American soul. Many times, he would request that I stay after school for counseling. Through his love and respect, I began to blossom once again.

After graduating from middle school, I spent the last summer in my village. Because our village did not have a high school, we filled out applications to attend Mount Edgecumbe or Sheldon Jackson, both in Sitka. At the advice of my grandfather Isaac, I filled out the application for Sheldon Jackson, which was a Christian high school. He told me it was a much better Indian boarding school, but when I learned all my eight-grade classmates were going to Mount Edgecumbe, I tore up my acceptance letter from Sheldon Jackson and filled out the application for Mount Edgecumbe.

After arriving at the Native American Indian School, reality began to settle in, and once again, I felt all alone. There was no church to attend, no Mr. Demmert for counseling, and no Christian Grandmother. I faced dull, gray dormitories with boring teachers.

Separated from parents and siblings and the native way of life, the unchallenged and lonely Native American students sought to fill the void and began to drink and party every opportunity they had. They would board the ferry from Mt. Edgecumbe to Sitka to find anyone who would sell them liquor. Hiding their vodka in their jacket pocket, they would go to their dorms, bring out the pints of liquor and get drunk. Then the racial wars would begin. Despite the fact that we were all from the tribes in Alaska, there was still racial tension, causing fist fights between the Tlingits against the Haidas, and the Aleutes against the Athabascians and Inupiat. I stood back and watched, wondering how could there be so much hatred among us brown people?

When the school year ended, my supervisor called my mother in for consultation and told her she must register me in another school. She said all my classes were not challenging enough for me and if I stayed, she would lose me to drug abuse. So Mom decided to move me to Juneau, the capital city of Alaska.

A Russian and a Tlingit

Walking down the hallway at Juneau High School, I observed *another* racial divide—this time between the whites and the Alaskan natives. I naturally gravitated to the native's side. Unsupervised and uncared for, I, too, started drinking. Soon I found I was not able to stop. I was a fifteen-year-old alcoholic.

During the first month at Juneau High, I met a strong, handsome Russian with deep blue eyes and a great sense of humor. I liked being with him because he always made me laugh, and he was kind to me. When our teachers saw us together, they tried to discourage our relationship because we were a mixed race, but we continued to go out on weekend dates. To keep the teachers from reading our love notes, we learned the Russian alphabet and printed our notes in that language. On one weekend, the police found us together drunk and put me in jail. Our probation officers suggested our separation, but we took every secret opportunity to be together.

When school closed for the summer, I continued to get into trouble with the law, so the court made the decision to send me to a home for troubled native youth in Fairbanks, Alaska. Before I was deported, Mike and I got together for the last time. As I boarded my flight to Fairbanks, my heart was breaking for the young man that I loved and had to leave behind.

Three months after arriving at the Fairbanks home, right after breakfast, I quietly went to the bathroom and threw up again, but this time one of the office staff heard me. After questioning me, they sent me to a doctor, and upon examination, found I was three-months pregnant. Because they were not a facility to accommodate live births, they quickly sent me to the Home of Unwed Mothers in Anchorage. Most of the girls living in that home were from the white well-to-do families who had secretly sent their daughters to the home to give birth and put their babies up for adoption. At that time, I was the only native living there. No one was overly friendly with me, so again I felt very alone.

After arriving at this home, my mother would periodically call, and in her drunken-slurred voice tell me to give my baby away, so we usually ended every phone call angry at each other. In all her phone calls, I do not remember her ever telling me she loved me. Toward the end of my pregnancy, the social workers called me into their office and advised me to sign papers to put my baby up for adoption. They told me repeatedly that I was too unstable to be a mother, but I ignored all their advice. I was confused and all alone with no one to talk to, so I just cried myself to sleep every night.

One morning, one of my roommates who was eight-months pregnant argued with me, saying horrible things to me about my pregnancy. When she referred to my sobbing, I do not know exactly *what* she said that caused my pent-up anger to explode, but I beat her so badly I put her in the hospital, causing her to give birth prematurely.

After that incident, my supervisor and social worker spoke with me again, telling me how unstable I was and how I needed to give my child to loving parents who would and could raise her better than I could. Again, I declined their offer, which seemed to anger them greatly.

It was now my ninth month, and my due date was approaching. For the last two weeks, this child was kicking and stretching, wanting to see the world. One afternoon, the baby twisted and I felt it now in position for birth. One early March day, just as I sat down to have lunch, I felt a twinge and then the contractions started. I let the staff know, and they told me to pack my belongings because I would not be returning to the home. They would fly me back to Juneau after the doctor discharged me. The home staff checked me into the hospital, and then they left me all alone with a nurse who put me in a room by myself! In all that time, no one came to check on me. After eight hours of hard labor, I was clutching the bed rails and screaming in pain and fear in this dark, empty room. Suddenly, the door opened and this fat nurse came barging in and screamed at me, "Shut up! SHUT UP! You're not the first one to have a baby!" Then she stormed out. An hour or so later, I gave birth to a precious little girl.

When I was well enough to travel, I flew back to Juneau. My mother met me and instantly bonded with her first grandchild. About a month or so later, my mom said she would watch my daughter, so I walked to the high school and made an appointment to speak with the principal. I sure did not want to talk to him because he was a joyless man whom we called *Black Mac*. I always enjoyed learning, so I had no choice but to speak with him about returning to the high school. I told him about my child and asked him if I could return to school. He reluctantly consented as long as I did not speak to anyone about my child. I agreed. I walked down the hallway looking for Mike, but I could not find him, so I went to the restroom and there were three white girls standing in front of the mirror putting on lipstick. When they saw me, they huddled together, started whispering, and snickering at me. The same feelings of humiliation I experienced when twelve years old welled up in me again, so I turned away from them, walked out of the restroom, out the front door of the school, and never looked back.

I went from business to business trying to get a job, but because I was only sixteen, no one would hire me. Some said I had to be eighteen to operate the cash machine, but I think that was an excuse. Frustrated, wondering where I was going to get money to buy milk and baby food, I stopped off at a local café and ordered a cup of coffee. When I took the first sip, I heard the door open and there was Mike walking toward me. He sat down next to me and my heart started doing flip-flops. He was still as handsome as I remembered him. He ordered a cup of coffee, turned,

57

and said to me, "I heard you had a daughter. I would like to see her."

I told him where I lived and said my mom would let him in. I went to the store, picked up some formula and other baby stuff, and hurried home. When I walked in the bedroom, Mike was gently holding our daughter in his lap with tears flowing unashamedly down his face. All my anger and confusion over Mike abandoning me melted away, and we were married four months later.

I Am Not Finished with Saturday Yet!

By the age of twenty, we had four beautiful daughters. I tried to be a good mother, but just like my own mother, something got hold of me and caught me in a vicious web of alcoholism and street drugs. Mike had his own challenges, and one challenge was struggling to find work for his family. When he did work, we would cash his check and use most of the money to go to the bars on Saturday night and get drunk. Toward the end of one school year, we had to send our two oldest girls to our next-door neighbor so they could feed them breakfast before they walked to school. We had no food in the cupboard. I still had a little self-respect left, so when Mike sent me down to the government office to ask for welfare, my face reddened with great shame. We only got one welfare check in all the years we raised our family, but it was one too many for me, for my grandmother raised me to be self-reliant and to work for what I wanted and needed.

One day, Grandpa called Mike and asked him if he wanted to bring his family down to Klawock to fish for just one summer. We jumped at the opportunity to make some money for our growing family. We packed up our belongings and flew to my village. Mike bought fishing gear from a store in Craig and went out to the fishing grounds with Grandpa. He would be gone for several days at a time. When they had their fish capacity, they would come home toward the weekend and unload their catch onto a processing vessel. Usually I met the boat and anxiously waited for Mike to get off to give him a big hug. On one occasion, I did not greet him but stayed home in bed.

When he finished unloading the fish, he came home that evening and found me moaning in pain. We did not have a doctor or nurse in our village, so I just suffered for days as quietly as I could, trying not to disturb anyone. By the time Mike arrived, the right side of my abdomen was tender to the touch, and I had a fever.

During that long night, the pain became so severe I was now screaming in agony. When the light of dawn peeked in the house, Mike brought a lighted lantern, and Grandma came into the bedroom. When Mike took a close look at me, he fell at my bedside, grabbed my hand, and started sobbing almost hysterically. Grandma stood in the doorway and started praying—at first softly—and then loudly. I whispered to Mike, "Why are you crying?" He said, "All around your eyes and mouth is pitch black!" Then Grandma moved closer to me. When she saw me, she yelled, "Florence, you're dying! Pray! Pray!"

Mike's crying and Grandma's booming voice began strangely trailing off as if my life was ebbing away. I did not have any more physical strength to fight the feeling any longer. I felt like I was slowly fading into nothingness when something jarred me alert, and I opened my eyes, blinked a couple of times trying to refocus. Grandma again yelled out to me, "Florence, you are dying. Pray!"

I was so weak I could barely lift my limp hand, but I raised it as far in the air as I could and meekly whispered, "Lord, if You will let me live, I will give my life to You." Instantly, the pain was gone!

Before I could fully take in what had just happened, we could hear helicopter blades whirling overhead as it slowly landed on the leveled school grounds. The medics quickly jumped out with a stretcher in hand and ran toward Grandma's house. They put me on the stretcher, then into the helicopter, and we flew the ninety miles to Ketchikan General where the surgeons did emergency surgery. I was in the hospital for a week and lost fifteen-to-twenty pounds.

Even though I was still very feeble, I was lonely for my family, and I was ready to go home. When discharged, I took a cab to the floatplane and paid for the next scheduled flight back to Klawock. I had an hour or so before I had to board, so I walked to the next building that was a bar and ordered a tall drink, completely forgetting the vow I had just made to the Lord on my deathbed. But Jesus had not forgotten.

Sunday's A'Coming!

For many years, I suffered the pain and shame of drug addiction until I ended up in a psychiatric ward in Anchorage. I was twenty-five years old, going on eighty-five. My body was broken and used up, my soul devoid of feeling except for hate, and my spirit black and empty. The doctors put me in a dorm and drugged me with anti-psychotic drugs to keep me from becoming violent. I had tried to kill four people, so it was a wise decision for the doctors to drug me. After I had been at the hospital for about three weeks, I had a night vision—a dream about hell and Jesus coming to rescue me. To read the full account of my salvation experience, please read my book, *Wind That Fans the Flame.*

After I was born again, I started attending Bethel Assembly of God with my family and we were the happiest we had ever been!

Mike and Flo on their 25th wedding aniversary. They have been married 50 years.

Flo in white buckskin dress.

61

Chapter 5

A DRUG-SOAKED MIND

"Hi Flo, this is Ramona. I am calling to see how you are. Is this a good time to talk?" As an older sister in the Lord, Ramona prayed for me from the time of my spiritual awakening and would periodically call and check on my well-being.

Holding the phone tightly to my ear, I replied, "Hi, Ramona, how nice to hear from you."

After a brief exchange of pleasantries she asked in her usual soft-spoken voice, "What are you doing?"

I responded with passionate enthusiasm, "I am writing to the Emperor of Ethiopia!" There was a brief silence then she repeated her question, "No, *really*, what are you doing?" I again responded, "I am writing to the Emperor of Ethiopia! He is persecuting Christians and many are suffering untold misery under his hand. He has even imprisoned some, killed and tortured others, so I am writing to him, saying, 'Let my people go!' "

Born Tafari Makonnen Woldemikael, the last emperor of Ethiopia changed his name to *Haile Selassie*, which means, "Might of the trinity." He traced his ancestral line back to Menelik I, who was credited with being the child of King Solomon of Israel and the Queen of Sheba. For four decades, he ruled by centralizing his own power, and in the 70s, at the end of his reign, his people were starving to death, while in his palace, his guests were dining in opulent luxury.

The old axiom, "Power corrupts, and absolute power corrupts absolutely" is evident in every leader who has not submitted to the rule of Jesus Christ and His Kingdom. He alone can guide with wisdom from above and help with the daily complex problems of any leader from a Native American chief to a president or an emperor. If Haile Selassie would have been *that* kind of leader, he could have led his people and his nation into prosperity and prominence and been hailed as one of the world's great leaders.

The same was true of Jimmy Carter. He told the Christian group, the *Moral Majority*, he was a born-again believer and won the Christian vote that helped put him in the office of the president of the United States. After sworn in as our president, I sent him a telegram and said something to this effect, "Mr. President, you ran on the fact that you are a born-again believer, and because of that position, you won our Christian vote. Therefore, I adjure you to publicly declare this fact to the nation who elected you as their president." I never heard back from him nor did he ever establish that fact publicly that I am aware of. I wonder what great legacy he would have left behind if he would have acknowledged and given all the praise to Jesus for putting him in that exalted position.

The Spirit of Your Mind

The greatest asset we have outside of Jesus Christ, His Word, and The Holy Spirit is our mind. With our mind and the help of the Holy Spirit, we can become a good leader and solve complex problems that affect our personal lives, our tribal government, and our nation's destiny.

Before I was born again, it seemed I was always trying to protect myself from physical, sexual, and mental harm. On one occasion, I was beaten and hit with a blunt instrument with such force that I suffered severe trauma to the head that affected my thinking pattern for years to come. However, the worse damage to my mind was spiritual. Whenever I took drugs, a demonic force would take over my mind, and I was as a little lamb led to the slaughter. The night I was born again, The Holy Spirit began His cleansing work in me. The desire for alcohol and all other addictions left me. Immediately, also my foul cursing stopped, which was so amazing to me and to those who knew me, for I was the daughter of a logger and I swore like one!

A month or so after I totally surrendered to Jesus as my Lord and Savior, Mike and I took our four daughters for a mountain hike. On the trail, I would pick up tiny flowers, marvel at their beauty, and wonder how I *never* noticed them before! My whole life had changed, and I was now fully alive as I took in the breath-taking wonder of the universe and the tiny little blue Forget-Me-Nots that guided us on the winding mountain path. As we were descending on our return home, my joy was suddenly gone when I was seized with this thought: *I don't know where I live*! I looked at Mike and told him, and he stared at me in disbelief. Slowly, ever so slowly, remembrance came to me of my home address. What a relief!

I continued to have bouts of forgetfulness, struggling with unseen forces trying to regain control of my mind. One day, this compelling thought came to me: *I am losing my mind.* It was a frightening moment. I stared wide-eyed at Mike and said, "Please take me to the hospital, I am losing my mind!" Mike immediately took me to the car, sped to the hospital, and parked near the emergency door. Just as he was opening my car door, this penetrating thought flooded my mind: *I have not given you a spirit of fear; but of power, and of love, and of a sound mind* (see 2 Timothy 1:7 KJV). At that time, I did not know where that thought came from. Was it from Scripture? I did not know. When I silently heard those words, I looked at Mike and said, "I don't need to go to the doctor. I am going to be just fine!" Mike just stared at me not expressing what he was thinking. Because I was a new believer in Christ, I did not know the Word of God, but the Holy Spirit of God, who wrote the Bible, knows the Word. He not only walks beside me, but He lives in me. He was the One who flooded my mind with that Scripture.

What Can Change My Anger?

I had been a born-again Christian for a few weeks when I was hired to work at an alcohol rehab facility. I was delighted to give back to the Lord for delivering me from drugs by helping others with similar problems. The clients appreciated my efforts to help them—especially when I worked the "graveyard" shift helping them while they were going through DTs. I enjoyed working with the medical staff with the exception of a middle-aged woman. She professed Christianity but, like all of us, she had some issues she was working on. One of her issues was bouts of jealousy against me for reasons unknown to me.

One day I heard she had gone to the head of our office and told lies about me. I was irate with her and confronted her in her office. My display of anger and caustic words toward her was not very Christ-like. I was so angry I was shaking. I was afraid if I did not leave; I would not be in control of my emotions, so I walked out of the office and to our church that was only two blocks away from my workplace. Stinging tears flowed down my face as I walked to the altar area. Thank God, my pastor was not in the church. I cried out, "Lord, why did I say those words to her? What is wrong with me? Why am I so angry all the time?" I looked down at the large open Bible on the "Do This In Remembrance of Me" altar table and Proverbs 15:1 was displayed: "A soft answer turns away wrath, but a harsh word stirs up anger. The tongue of the wise uses knowledge rightly, but the mouth of fools pours forth foolishness" (NIV).

Reading those words of life brought tears of repentance and deliverance from my anger that day. Oh, there were many times over the past forty-two years I have acted unbecomingly, but each time the Holy Spirit would have me go back, apologize, and ask for forgiveness for my behavior. Moreover, each time I responded appropriately to Him, He bought great joy and peace to my soul.

Jesus Walks into My Room

The nurses rolled me out of surgery and into my room. When I awoke from the anesthesia, I was hearing ugly voices in my head. What is going on? When one of my family members would ask me a question, their voice was interrupted by another voice in my mind, and I would answer the voice in my head! My family would have this puzzled look and then walk out of the room. I asked my doctor why this was happening and he said he did not have an answer.

My closest friend, Kathie, was also a nurse at the Juneau Hospital, so I spoke to her about this frightening experience. She was very concerned for me, so she decided to stay after visiting hours to intercede for me. She told me as she was praying for me, with her eyes shut, she heard the door open. When she looked up, to her surprise, no one was there! The next morning, to my joy and relief, I no longer heard those voices. Jesus had come to my hospital room and delivered me Himself! Hallelujah.

Forgive Your Mother-in-law

Each spring, my mother-in-law would invite our family for her delicious Russian Easter Brunch, but this year our girls were all grown up and had a family of their own, so it was just Mike and me for Sunday brunch.

My mother-in-law was a strong, independent Russian. She loved to tell stories and laugh, but infrequently, she became depressed and withdrawn. During those bouts of sadness, she displayed bitterness because of a very troubling childhood and her first marriage that ended in failure in a court battle. However, underneath her hard exterior, she was a kind and loving person. She attended a religious church, but she did not have a personal relationship with Jesus Christ. I was always finding ways to show her Jesus' love so that she would give her life to Him, but she always resisted me. I was very concerned for her welfare because she was getting older, and I did not want her to pass from this life without knowing Him.

After we had our beautiful Easter lunch, I started to share with her about Jesus when, all of a sudden, she stood up violently. Trembling, she began to scream the foulest things to me, hidden things now expressed with deep animosity. Mike and I were in shock at this outburst of such intense hatred for me. Finally, Mike tried to calm her down, but she continued her tirade,

69

so Mike grabbed our coats and we quickly left. Mike had come to his mother's house after I had arrived, so we both had our own vehicle. As we stood in front of my car, he put his arms around me and apologized for her, and then he just wept. He said he would see me at home, but he was gone for hours. He was trying to sort it all out, but he was so confused and deeply hurt. She never called or spoke to him for two years after that incident.

While ministering at a Washington State Bible Training School, I received word my mother-in-law, Tillie, was dying, so I contacted two dear friends of mine, Drs. Al and Margaret Martin, who knew her when they all attended the same church. However, my friends did not stay in that religion after they were born-again. I told them how much I loved my mother-in-law (and they did too), and I wanted her to say the sinner's prayer before she departed this life. They agreed to go and see her.

After ministering words of life to her, they led her in the sinner's prayer and left with the assurance that she was truly born-again. However, the next day, the Holy Spirit spoke to my friends and told them to go back and speak to her one more time. When they were at her bedside, they told her the Lord told them to come back to make sure she had forgiven everyone who had ever hurt her. She agreed to pray with them once again.

After they finished praying, my friend, Margaret, said to Tillie, "The Lord wants you to forgive one more person, your daughter-in-law, Flo Ellers." They acted as if they did not know me, so it was easier

70

for my mother-in-law to forgive. She repeated the prayer and the forgiveness was complete. A few days later, she went home to be with Jesus—free from all bitterness and hate. I know when the angels took her, she had an abundant entrance through heaven's gate into the presence of her Lord and Savior.

My Mother Is Not My Problem?

In those early days of my newfound faith in Jesus Christ, I had such joy in getting to know Him and His great love for me. With every battle, He was by my side, helping me to come out on the other side into His glorious victory. One morning I awoke feeling very sad. Intuitively, I knew I was about to go through what was one of the last battles with my mind. As the day progressed, this depression went deeper than I had ever experienced. I became very concerned that I would not be able to come back from the dark pit I was sinking into, so I made an appointment with a psychiatrist. At that time in my life, I did not know how to resist the Enemy, so I retreated to the only recourse I thought I had, the medical community.

During my first appointment, the psychiatrist asked me to explain why I had come to her. I began by telling her what I was experiencing about the long, dark shadows of my past trying to drag me back. Then the conversation went to my mother. I told her how my mother did bad things to me. I was becoming very agitated, blaming her for all my problems in life when the doctor abruptly said to me, "Flo, I want you to tell me _your_ problem, and I want you to stop right now putting the blame on your mother."

71

Her comment shocked me back to reality, and I finished my hour with her and never made another appointment. After returning home, I thought about what she said to me and realized the Holy Spirit was the one speaking to me through her. He showed me why I was so angry at life by blaming all my problems on my mother. The Lord helped me to repent of my wrong attitude and from that day forward, I began to take responsibility for my own actions, which dramatically altered my life and affected my future in a positive way. I never went back to the mental community again, knowing my only help comes from the Lord.

A couple of years after my life dramatically changed, my mother also gave her heart and life in total surrender to Jesus. She was not only my beloved mother but she became my best friend too. At the end of every phone conversation, she would always say to me, "I love you, Flo." Even in her dying breath, she told me she loved me. Those words healed my troubled soul and freed me to love others.

Tripartite Being

Of all God's creations, man is the only one who is a tripartite being, which means he has a spirit, a soul, and a body. However, an animal has only a body and soul, which separates us from the animals, birds, and reptiles. When you give your life over to Jesus, He gives *life* to your dead spirit and you become what the Bible calls a "born-again" fully alive spirit (see John 3:1-21).

Your spirit, joined to His Spirit, can now hear God's voice speaking to you from within your being. Every word you hear from God will be beautiful thoughts, and you can back up His words from the Bible. God will not speak to you anything that is contrary to His Word.

When you hear Him, you receive those thoughts first in your spirit-man, flowing to your brain. You now have a conscious thought of what your spirit-man heard.

One of the benefits of being born-again and knowing God is having a sound mind, which is a mind free from any and all damage, so you can have self-control and valid reasoning. That is why the demon attacks your mind because if he can get into your thoughts, he has you! He can deceive you into believing a lie. Staying in the Word *daily*, Bible memorization, and Christian fellowship will keep you from his beguiling thoughts that lead only to deception and ultimately, death.

There is no substitute for light, love, and life! God's Word—the Bible—will take you from depression into His peace, from trouble to deliverance, from dilemma to solution, from failure to victory, from defeat to a life full of goodness, kindness, and overwhelming joy. Proverbs 7:1-5 says, "My son, keep my words, and treasure my commands within you. Keep my commands and live, and my law as the apple of your eye. Bind them on your fingers; write them on the tablet of your heart. Say to wisdom, 'You are my sister,' and call understanding your nearest kin, that they may keep you from the immoral woman, from the seductress who flatters with her words."

Chapter 6

TIPPECANOE MASSACRE

I have always liked order. When Grandma sewed bags for our clothing, I made certain socks were in one bag and underwear in another bag and hung up on the wall. Even though we did not have chest of drawers for our clothes, I still attempted to decorate my bedroom as nicely as I could beautify it with what I had. After I grew up and gave my heart and life to Jesus, my desire for neatness transferred to Kingdom order. I recognized early in my Christian development there are absolutes in God's Word and there is a wrong way and a right way to approach life.

I had finally finished decorating our house we had recently purchased after our move to Ketchikan, Alaska. The coordinated color scheme was stylish with our newly framed Alaskan prints on the wall and beautiful new furniture in the sitting room arranged in "Kingdom order." I gave myself a nod of approval as I looked over my home. Now I was ready to "play house." Only one thing left to do—wash the goat head.

Mike was a hunter and he liked to have his trophies mounted so he could admire them when he sat in his living room chair. One of his favorites was his mounted goat head. I hammered in the last of the decorator hooks so I could hang it, but when I looked at the stuffed head, it looked dirty to me. I got the bottle of shampoo, put the head under the running faucet just as I used to do with my girls, squirted on a generous amount of shampoo, and started scrubbing the head vigorously. The bubbles were floating in the air as I rinsed it. I wiped it with a towel and hung it up on the wall.

It was lunchtime and Mike would be home soon. I had been working hard all morning, so I thought I would take a five-minute break before he came home. I sat in Mike's chair and looked over at my handy work. To my horror, the glue had softened and the goat's ears were hanging down. Just as I opened my mouth and gasped, the back door opened and Mike came in with a big smile on his face. He always liked my cooking and loved to come home for lunch. When he looked at me with his big grin, I tried to hide my expression, but I never could hide my true feelings. He narrowed his eyes and asked, "What did you do, Flo?" I slowly turned my head to the wall where his favorite goat head was hanging, and he followed my movement. We both stared in silence at the dead head, watching the water run down the wall and the goat's ears slowly falling off!

My Kitchen Work and God's Work

After Mike returned to work, I turned on the TV, went to the kitchen, and began to wash the dishes. My work was interrupted when the newscaster said with a loud but shaky voice, "President Reagan has just been shot!" I stopped what I was doing and ran into the family room and turned up the volume as he repeated the story. The Holy Spirit within me said in a commanding voice, "Call the intercessors and tell them to pray!" I got on the phone, called my friends Clarine, Mary, and Lynda, and told them to call the next line of intercessors that they knew, and I quickly hung up the phone. I ran back to the family room to pray. Then, the reporter said, "The President has *not* been shot . . ." but I heard in my spirit man, "The President *has* been shot, keep praying!" After about a half hour, the conflicting report confirmed President Reagan was shot and scheduled for immediate surgery. For about five hours, I continued in deep intercession for him. When I sensed a release in my spirit man, I stopped praying.

A few days later, all the nation watched as President Reagan, clothed in his dark blue robe with his arm around his wife, Nancy, waved at the waiting crowd below his hospital window. We were all so relieved to know our beloved president was alive and well.

The Curse on the Presidents

At the time of the shooting, most Christians were aware of Tecumseh's brother, "The prophet" who put a curse on the presidency. The prophet's curse was every twenty years after President Harrison, the president elected in a zero year would die in office. President Reagan, elected in 1980, was a zero-year president, and it seemed he broke that curse, or did he?

Several months after this terrible incident, a well-known television talk-show host interviewed Mrs. Reagan about the attempted assignation on her husband. She asked, "What did you feel; what did you go through when you finally learned the truth that your husband had been shot?" Mrs. Reagan shared her feelings of trepidation as she faced the uncertainly of her husband's outcome in the surgery room. After a couple more minutes of sharing, Mrs. Reagan then began to tell the audience the most compelling part of her testimony. She said when President Reagan regained consciousness after his surgery, he told Nancy Jesus Christ appeared to him just moments before his sedation for surgery. He told Nancy that Jesus said to him, "If you will forgive the man who shot you, I will let you live." President Reagan said to his wife he had a moment's hesitation and then told the Lord in a whisper, "I forgive him," and he said immediately he felt life returning to him.

78

Dr. B.L. Rice, Shalom Bible College, W. Des Moines, Iowa; Flo Ellers; Jeff Johns, Pastor, White Horse Christian Center, West Lafayette, Indiana

Tecumseh's Brother's Word Curse

It was a bitter cold November day in 1999, which is typical weather for that time of year in Indiana. Pastor Jeff from White Horse Christian Center (WHCC) in West Lafayette, Indiana, had invited me to speak at his yearly November Prophetic Conference.

During the day and in between the scheduled meetings, he seemed intent on showing me two specific areas: one was a battlefield by Tippecanoe River where 900 Shawnee warriors were slaughtered, and the other was a monument he had found hidden on a hill overlooking that battleground. He first drove us to the place where the great conflict occurred between Chief Tecumseh's warriors and then Governor William Harrison. After this showing, he asked me if I would like to join him and five other intercessors the following morning to the monument site he had discovered. I agreed and the next day early

79

in the morning, their van came for me. We drove to the hill where he had made this exciting discovery. We all piled out of the van and began to struggle to get up a rocky hill overgrown with tall bushes. Out of breath, we came to a clearing and there was the hidden monument to Tecumseh's brother called "The Prophet." He asked us to pray and I walked over to the monument that overlooked the huge valley below where the battle took place.

As I began to pray for my people, the Native American, suddenly, I could feel in my spirit the same intense hatred for the white man *they* had felt as I identified with them in intercession. At that time animosity like that was a foreign feeling to me because I no longer felt such hatred toward my white brothers and sisters. When I concluded my prayer, I tagged on this request, "Lord, raise up *Your* prophets from among our people who will speak the truth— *Your* Truth to my people." In silence, we left that place and I went back to my hotel room.

A Very Important Date in History

The next day, a friend from WHCC asked if I would like to visit their local museum. I consented, which I found interesting because I really do *not* like to do anything outside of the meetings. I would rather stay focused on what the Lord is doing and saying; yet, I felt impressed to go with her. She picked me up and drove me to the local West Lafayette Museum. I was drawn to the murals and the photos that told the story about the battle between Harrison and Tecumseh's brother that occurred on November 7, 1811. The Holy

Spirit seemed to add particular emphasis to that date. Here is the story of that battle.

There was building resentment between the great Shawnee Chief Tecumseh and Governor William Henry Harrison of Indiana. Tecumseh was a visionary, military strategist and had keen insight to what Governor Harrison was attempting to do as he made an agreement with the Indians for their land. Governor Harrison gave the Indians whiskey and bribed them to sign a treaty to cede three million acres of their lands to the U. S. Government! Chief Tecumseh saw this as a hostile act and decided to organize the tribes to end the conflict of who was the rightful owner of the land.

Tecumseh left his brother, Tenskwatawa, the religious sage, called The Prophet of his tribe, in charge of his warriors and rode off to form a confederacy of the plains and northern tribes. If Tecumseh were successful in his strategy to unify all the tribes, he would have concentrated power to stop Harrison. While he was gone, his brother, the prophet, had a dream about a war between Harrison and his people, and he shared it with the Shawnee warriors. He shared his dream telling them when we go into battle with Harrison and they shoot at us with their rifles, their bullets will not penetrate us or affect us. The elders made battle plans around their council fire and prepared for war.

81

However, Governor Harrison had plans of his own. Harrison and his army of 1,000 highly trained U.S. soldiers camped nearby Prophetstown where the prophet and his warriors with their families set up their tents by the Tippecanoe River. Tensions continued to escalate between Harrison and the prophet. Because of the arguments and mounting anger between them, nothing could quell the inevitable battle that ensued. Because of the prophet's dream of "divine" protection, Tecumseh's warriors did not fight *Indian style* but rushed headlong at Harrison's rifles, and 900 Shawnee warriors were easily defeated that day. On the hill, overlooking Prophetstown, the prophet and two other Shawnee leaders watched in horror the slaughtered warriors and Prophetstown burned.

Tecumseh's efforts to coalesce the tribes were nearly successful. When he returned with a strategic plan to defeat Governor Harrison, Chief Tecumseh heard about the massacre and fell into defeat. His well-laid plans were now in disarray, and all hope gone. He was livid with his brother and in anger told him to leave the camp. Scorned and disgraced, Tenskwatawa, the prophet, with his small band roamed the Northwest and Canada for several years. Chief Tecumseh and a few of his warriors attempted to make *peace with honor* with Governor Harrison, but Harrison would not relent, so Tecumseh joined the British

and in a heated battle with U. S. soldiers,
the great Shawnee Chief Tecumseh died.

The Massacre that Took Harrison to Washington D. C.

Because of his military prowess and victory at Prophetstown, Harrison was nicknamed, "Old Tippecanoe." He made a decision to run for president of the United States and asked John Tyler to run on the same ticket with him. Their slogan was "Tippecanoe and Tyler too!" The campaign began and Harrison used the massacre of Tecumseh's warriors as his political strategy to take him to the White House. In 1840, the newly elected Harrison became the ninth president of the United States.

After the death of Chief Tecumseh, his brother the prophet returned from Canada and pronounced a curse on the White House. He said, in essence, "You think I have lost my powers. I tell you I have *not* lost my power! When Harrison goes to the White House, he will die and after him, every Great Chief chosen every twenty years will die in office. Moreover, when each Great Chief dies, let everyone remember the death of our people."

President William Henry Harrison's Inauguration Day was cold and windy, but he refused to wear a coat. His speech lasted two hours, and when he retired to his new White House, he was chilled and tired. He contracted pneumonia and one month later, died in office. Thereafter, six more presidents elected in a zero year also died in office: Abraham

Lincoln, 1860; James A. Garfield, 1880; William McKinley, 1900; Warren G. Harding, 1920; Franklin D. Roosevelt, 1940; and John F. Kennedy, 1960. There was an attempted assignation on President Reagan in 1980, but it failed because he forgave his perpetrator. The next in line for the continuation of the "Zero Year Curse" was George W. Bush, elected on November 7, 2000.

The Curse Is Broken

Tensions mounted as our nation was divided between Al Gore, who won the popular vote and George W. Bush, who won the electoral votes. I was in West Lafayette, Indiana for another prophet's conference at WHCC. I was staying at my friend's home, Missionary Janet McArthur, who also attended that church. She gave me permission to use her computer, so I looked at the national news and then read my emails. I opened one email from Gwen Shaw, president and founder of End Time Handmaidens and Servants, an intercessory ministry, based out of Jasper, Arkansas. She was calling for all intercessors to pray for the nation's election and to pray specifically for George W. Bush. I forwarded the Prayer Alert to those from WHCC and continued to intercede for our nation.

While in prayer, the Holy Spirit highlighted today's date, which was November 7, 2000. He then spoke to me about the Battle of Tippecanoe. My mind began to go down the corridor of time as He showed me again the photos and the mural in the West Lafayette Museum. He then highlighted the date of that

horrific battle: November 7, 1811. He reminded me
of the three chiefs who overlooked the Tippecanoe
Massacre. Slowly the light dawned on me what He
was revealing, so I called the church office and asked
if I could meet with Pastor Jeff. When I entered his
office, there were two other church prophets and
one of the conference speakers, Bob Shattles, seated.
Pastor Jeff asked me what was so urgent, so I began
to explain the following outline of events:

- "The prophet" and Harrison's battle on
  November 7, 1811

- Today's date is November 7, 2000

- George W. Bush now in line for the "Zero Year
  Curse"

- There were three Shawnee warriors
  overlooking the battle

- We have _only_ three Native Americans here
  today: Bob Shattles, Bill Kallappa, and me

- End Time Handmaidens and Servants have
  called for a day of fasting for the president

- This is a prophet's conference.

After I finished enumerating and connecting the
dots of the unusual events past and current, Pastor
Jeff thought for a minute, and then asked me, "What
do you think we are supposed to do about this?"

I exclaimed with great passion, "Break the curse!"

He again looked at me, and said, "Flo, during tonight's service, you will be the one to break the curse!"

I said with a questioning look on my face, "Why me?"

Pastor Jeff said firmly, "Because the Holy Spirit showed you all these facts and put it together for you."

I was not happy at all about his decision. I did not feel qualified to break the curse, but I acquiesced to his leadership. All of us left and went back to our homes and continued the fasting and intercession for the newly elected president.

It was now time to go to the church for the evening's service. The praise was unusually strong and solemn as it penetrated the heavens and the adoration was very holy when we worshiped before God's Throne. When the music ended, Pastor Jeff went to the pulpit and told those who had gathered what had transpired that day. He said to the congregation, "We are going to break Tecumseh's brother's curse off the presidency." He added to the stunned audience if they were not in agreement with this that they could leave quietly and return when we were finished with the Lord's work. No one moved.

Jeff said to the ushers, "Close all the doors and lock them! No one is to go out or come in until we have concluded the Lord's business. Flo, Bob, and Bill, come to the platform." (We were the three "chiefs," but I did not feel like a chief!) Very reverently, we went to the platform and stood in quiet worship.

At the bidding of the Pastor and the Lord, I slowly walked to the pulpit and waited for the Holy Spirit to give me His words and the unction to pray. It seemed like an eternity of silence, but I am sure it was only a few seconds. With a strong commanding sound, we all began to pray in the Spirit in the Mighty Name of Jesus. Then, with all my faith, I yielded to the Holy Spirit as He spoke His command through me, and we broke the curse.

Chapter 7

THE PROCLAMATION
OF FORGIVENESS

In 1995, Reverend John and Anne Gimenez were guests of Paul and Jan Crouch on the Trinity Broadcasting Network, a Christian-owned TV ministry based in Southern California. In Jan's typical childlike manner, she asked Pastor John Gimenez why he was planning a second "Washington for Jesus" event on the Mall in Washington, D. C. He said the Lord spoke to him to organize the event to combat seven giants stalking the land, seeking to destroy a generation. He further declared that the Holy Spirit gave him the acronym for the word, *pharaoh*, for the seven giants. The seven giants were persecution of Christians, homosexuality, abortion, racism, addiction, occultism, and HIV/AIDS. After he presented some of the details, he gave a phone number for those interested in helping with the planning committee for this great gathering of Christians.

The next day, I called the number and the receptionist put me in touch with the coordinator of the planned event. I asked him who were some of the speakers, and he mentioned the names of many well-known ministers who would represent a few of the major ethnic groups and combat the seven giants. When he finished, I said to him. "Sir, in your roster of names representing the ethnic groups, you do not have *one* Native American on your list. You mean to tell me you are planning a major event in America and you have left out the host people of this great nation?"

There was a painful silence. Then he asked me, "Are *you* Native American?" I did not expect our conversation to go in this direction. I answered haltingly, "Well, yes I am."

"Well then, *you* will be our Native American representative! We are having a planning session and I would like to invite you to participate in this meeting."

I was speechless, but after a brief moment, I said quietly, "I will be there."

I flew to the East Coast and went to the planning session. At the conclusion of the meeting, the committee chair told us as a "Washington for Jesus Representative," we would have exactly ten minutes to address the nation on any of the seven giants given to Pastor Gimenez.

I left the meeting thinking, *What in the world was I thinking when I called the committee chairperson?* Now, I was really backed into a corner, so I decided to get out of my dilemma. I called a minister friend of mine and told Reverend Jody Brady what I had done and asked for her help. Reverend Brady was a missionary to the Apaches in Arizona, and I knew if anyone could articulate and address one of the giants, it would be her. Jody agreed to take my place, but before I could call the committee chairperson later that week, she called me back and told me the Lord said *I* was to address the nation. I was very disappointed about her decision, but I did not have an option. I fearfully put it in the Lord's hands and went to my next scheduled meetings, trying to put it out of my mind.

Off to Washington

Two days before the scheduled April 29-30, 1996, "Washington for Jesus" event, I left Alaska and stayed in Seattle overnight before I was to catch my flight to Washington D.C. I was staying in a home with a woman who was caring for several children. All I could hear was the happy chatter of their voices as they played and tackled one another in the living room. I tried to block out their noise and began to pray. I said, "Lord, in two days I will be given a unique opportunity to address this nation on the subject of Native American racism, and I do not have *one* thing to say! Furthermore, TBN is airing it on their TV network! Lord, I feel so inadequate, so small; please help me." I waited a few moments for Him to respond, and words started coming to me so I grabbed a pen and started to write "The Proclamation of Forgiveness."

91

When I arrived at the Washington Mall, several hundred thousand Christians from the nation had gathered in the rain to hear each speaker's plea and to pray for our nation's sins. It was now my turn, so an usher came with a large black umbrella to get me from the "green room," which was really a small silver trailer that housed the speakers. As we walked from the trailer in the rain, the presence of God came upon both of us and we started trembling; so he whispered, "Hold my arm." I do not know if he was trying to hold me upright or if he was asking me to help him walk in a dignified manner, which was appropriate for the event.

We walked in silence as we looked across the vast audience of hundreds of thousands of Christians and a few reporters. There was a holy hush over the mall. It felt like I was in a church service surrounded by a heavenly host of angels. The usher escorted me to the covered platform, and I took out my scribbled notes and began to proclaim what I had written down. With each sentence, I could hear an echo, the feedback from the huge speakers, so I had to wait until the echo faded before I spoke the next sentence. Because of the hesitation between sentences, it gave the full import the Lord wanted as the audience listened and weighed the words. When I got past the first paragraph, I could sense someone's strong presence behind me on the platform and I knew if this was not being aired on national TV that person, whoever it was, would have had me removed from the platform. When I finished, I could barely walk because the anointing or the power of the Christ was so strong on me. I could not stay at the mall, but I went immediately back to my hotel room, fell on my knees, and wept profusely before the Lord.

Second Visit to Washington D. C.

Nine years after I delivered that proclamation, I sensed I was to try to deliver a copy of it to President Bush. Reverend Jody Brady, who knew Senator Greenleaf of Pennsylvania, asked for his help. He got me the presidential appointment, not with President Bush but with his deputy assistant, Mr. Ruben Barrales, Director of Intergovernmental Affairs. The meeting was set for October 4, 2005, which fell on the Jewish holiday of Rosh Hashanah.

With the scheduled appointment in place, I contacted a couple of Native American chiefs and we put together a team of six other Native American pastors and evangelists to go with me. The team consisted of Reverend George M. Kallappa Sr. from the Makah Tribe; G. Anne Richardson, Chief of the Rappahannock Tribe; Reverend Ivan Doxtator, Oneida of the Iroquois Confederacy; Reverend Linda S. Doxtator, Cherokee; Evangelist Glen W. Anniskette, Tlingit; Reverend Dewey Kirstein, III, Cherokee; and me of the Tlingit and Cherokee Tribes.

We arrived in our nation's capital and spent the night in prayer before going to the Eisenhower Building to meet with Mr. Ruben Barrales. I was very disappointed that we were not meeting with President Bush but grateful for the open door. We were all a little nervous as we went through security screening and were led to Mr. Barrales' office. Given five minutes to present his or her words for the president, each team member spoke to Mr. Barrales with great eloquence. I was righteously proud of each one of them. When their five minutes were up, each gave a native gift representing his or her tribe. Mr. Barrales listened respectfully and accepted graciously each gift.

Lastly, it was my turn to speak. I felt strongly impressed to stand up as I began to speak to Mr. Barrales. I thanked him for meeting with us and said, "You are sitting in proxy for our nation's chief, so I will address you as if you were the president of our nation. Our team represents the Native Christian community, and we have come here to declare forgiveness on behalf of our people in the name of Jesus."

As I began to read the Proclamation, I almost lost my composure when I read the part about our government stripping our people of their dignity. Slightly shaken, I lifted the heavily framed document and began to read:

"PROCLAMATION OF FORGIVENESS"

Presented to

The Honorable George Walker Bush, President of the United States

"The earth is the Lord's and everything in it, the world and all who live in it." (Psalms 24:1 NIV)

How blessed are the people whose God is the Lord.

The earth is the Lord's by right of Creation. His absolute sovereignty precludes our right to determine our own destiny. Our purpose for being is with the God who has created us all

ONE NATION UNDER GOD . . .

In Christopher Columbus' traveling diary, he said as he approached this land, "I was blown by the Wind of God." Columbus came with a holy ambition to establish a nation where Christian liberty would prevail, but others who came did not all have a purity of heart. With force, they used their _long knives_ to take the wealth of the land, the temptation before them too powerful to resist. A brown-eyed people unable to defend their land and their families were consumed in the greed of the settlers from Europe. What would have been the ultimate outcome of this nation had the early settlers wholly followed the Puritan's one desire for religious freedom?

ONE NATION UNDER GOD . . .

What would this nation be like today if our forefathers had resisted the proud attempt to take destiny into their own hands and seize the reigns of history?

ONE NATION UNDER GOD . . .

What would this nation be like today had the early pioneers been willing to present the Gospel to the Native American Indians and to lift _them_ up out of their

95

spiritual darkness to serve the Living God?

ONE NATION UNDER GOD . . .

Instead, their lust for the gold in the land promoted acts of aggression on territories, which were not their own. The encroachments were a willful violation of the Word of God that says, "Do not remove the ancient landmark" (Proverbs 23:10).

The bows and arrows, the hunting knives, and the tomahawk were no match for the Remington rifles. A once proud people had to bow into submission as acre after acre was forcefully taken from them. What would this nation be like if all the races could have dwelt together in harmony sharing the land and its vast resources?

ONE NATION UNDER GOD . . .

Deceptive governmental leaders said, "Let's make covenant with these people. They are too naïve and could not possibly understand the ramifications of these treaties." So one by one, a treaty was drawn up, and one by one each of the 372 treaties were violated and broken. The intense hatred of the governmental leaders released orders for the genocidal eradication of the Red Man. The pony soldier's pet-saying was, "The only good Indian is a dead Indian." The historic massacres amounted to over 50 million! The buffalo by the thousands lay slaughtered across the land, the once defiant

Native American Indian blood soaked up the ground, and the land became defiled and cursed. O America, America, in the midst of all of this, God shed His Grace on thee. He brought you here for His eternal purpose—to bring religious freedom to this nation and the nations of the world. Your mandate from Him was for you to propagate the nations with the Gospel from your stately posture and you were to begin with First Nations people, but you have never fulfilled your mandate from God. Instead, you force marched them onto reservations and all their dignity was stripped from them. All hope for a future was gone. Their blood is crying out for restitution. We have sown to the wind, and we have reaped the whirlwind. If our nation is to be changed, our national sin must be recognized, acknowledged, and repented of and then we can be

ONE NATION UNDER GOD . . .

There was another Man whose blood was also shed. He was the Man from heaven, the very Son of God who came in the flesh approximately 2,000 years ago. He lived among men and healed all their hurts and diseases; and when His blood splattered that ole' rugged cross, He never cried out for revenge but said, "Father, forgive them. . . ." Our shed blood cries out one message; His blood cries out another message. Therefore, we as Native American Indian Christian representatives of the host people of this great nation, make this proclamation to President George W. Bush, The Congress, and other national leaders that we forgive our nation and its leaders for what they have done to us in the past. We believe if you will accept this Proclamation of Forgiveness, we will see and experience a mighty outpouring of God's Presence that will affect all of the United States of America and then we will truly be

ONE NATION UNDER GOD.

Signed on October 4, 2005, by seven Native American representatives and Mr. Ruben Barrales, Deputy Assistant to the President; Director of Intergovernmental Affairs; The White House.

When I finished reading the proclamation, most of us had tears in our eyes. I presented the framed document (fit for a president) to Mr. Barrales (a Catholic) who looked at it and said, "Oh, you had it framed. I am impressed." Then he asked if he could give me a hug! We all embraced and held hands as a symbol of our unity and prayed a powerful prayer for President Bush and our great nation.

The electrified atmosphere of the presence of the Lord was glorious as Mr. Barrales responded by thanking each of us for our words and gifts. For the group of seven Native Americans, it became memorable and forever etched in our hearts and minds. This small band of Indian leaders to have gone to the White House to address the Nation's

Chief and say to him, "We forgive our nation for what they have done to us in the past," expressed the very heart of God. I believe Heaven recorded this act, and we now wait to see the fruit of our grand visit.

After the meeting with Mr. Barrales, his assistant escorted us to the Treaty Room on the fourth floor of the Eisenhower Building! In this room, our government wrote the treaties; and in this room, before the ink dried, they were subsequently broken between the Red Man and the U.S. Government. In each of our own way, we circled the room praying in whispers only the Holy Spirit heard. We left the Treaty Room in silence completely undone by the Lord's presence and thanking Him for such a holy moment in our nation's history.

Dr. Flo Ellers; Rev. Dewey Kirstein, III; Rev. George M. Kallappa; Chief G. Anne Richardson; Mr. Ruben Barrales; Rev. Linda S. Doxtator; Rev. Ivan Doxtator; Rev. Glen W. Anniskette.

Chapter 8

REDEEMING THE LAND

While brushing my teeth, I heard something similar to these words, "You will be asked to help establish a church with a small band of Hispanics, and you are to agree."

I responded, "I rebuke you, devil! Leave me." When I said that I thought those words came from an evil source, but it really was the Lord speaking to me. After hearing that instruction, a very brief time elapsed when my phone rang. One of the leaders of this Hispanic group, Rich Massiatt, was asking if I would help them start a church. I agreed, but only because I heard those words from the Lord. For three months, I taught them the Word of God regarding the church under divine government and spiritual principles they were to use to govern the people. They were a very easy group of believers to work with because they have a very enthusiastic spirit and a willing heart to work. After the Holy Spirit chose the elders and they were set in place, I had only one more teaching to give them before I drove back to Alaska.

Mike loved living in Livermore, California, for the winter months but the summer work season was approaching, so he reluctantly packed his belongings and drove back to Juneau. He allowed me to stay to finish the work in the newly formed church, True Vine Fellowship. (Several years after the church formed the leaders moved the church from Livermore to Tracy, California.)

In my last teaching, I taught them spiritual warfare principles outlined in *Redeeming the Land*, a book by Dr. Gwen Shaw. When I finished, twelve disciples volunteered to participate in a specific prayer strategy over the city of Livermore. In groups of four, each group went to the four points of the city. Each leader chose their area and I was designated the East, which included the Lawrence Livermore Laboratory (LLL)—a research and developmental institute of science, applied to national security. (You know, thermonuclear reaction, i.e. fusion . . . star wars, etc.) When we drove up to the LLL, immediately, armed security guards came to the wired gate and commanded us to move at least 300 feet away, so we quickly obeyed but we did not leave the area because we had instructions from the Lord to pray over this strategic point.

Each team leader took Communion elements and anointing oil with them. After they arrived at their destination, the leaders served Holy Communion to each warrior/intercessor, and then prayed over their designated areas, anointing them with oil. After we arrived at our section of the city by the LLL, I prayed, using the scriptural reference in Judges 4:21 when Jael took a tent peg and drove it in the enemy's temple (and used it to spiritually and symbolically represent doing "nailing" a wrong mindset). I asked the Lord to expose the enemy's schemes in the minds of those who work at this lab. After our prayer strategy, we regrouped and each leader gave a glorious report.

The next morning I awoke early and heard the Lord say to me, "I will show you what transpired as the result of your prayers over this city." I waited all day but nothing of interest was revealed to me. However, the second morning I awakened to a loud thud at the front door, and the Lord told me to go and get the newspaper. I ran quickly, picked it up, and opened it to the headlines that read, "Lawrence Livermore Lab Worker." I excitedly scoured the short article. It said a worker from LLL went to the local police station at 7 a.m. confessing several counts of sexual abuse against minors. They asked him why he voluntarily confessed to the crimes, and he said he was a Christian and the Lord spoke to him and told him to turn himself in to the police! It was the very next morning after we did the redeeming of the land prayer strategy!

With my work completed, I said my goodbyes to the leaders of the church, drove hundreds of miles from California to northern British Columbia, and put my car onto the ferry for Juneau.

Three weeks after I left California arriving in Juneau, I received an invitation to minister in a nearby Alaskan village. Packing an overnight bag, I caught a small commuter plane to my destination. After I unpacked, I turned on CNN for the top news and to my amazement, the reporter was standing outside of Lawrence Livermore Laboratory right where we had taken Holy Communion and anointed the ground. He was telling the TV audience how a 120-man drug ring was discovered at the LLL. I could hardly believe what I was hearing! I thought, *What would have happened in that nuclear laboratory if the Lord had not exposed that drug ring*? What a frightening thought! Thank God, The Holy Spirit knew what was going on behind those secured gates! He was the One who inspired our group to pray, using the Biblical reference of the Jael incident as our prayer strategy to expose the drug ring. To our Lord Jesus Christ is all the glory!

Redeeming the Land in Africa

I boarded my flight at London Heathrow for Nigeria, buckled my seat and snuggled in for the long flight to Lagos. I felt challenged when I received the invitation to preach and teach the Word of God to this large church of thousands in Lagos. When I arrived at the airport, the pastor met me, along with her elders who gave me the "red-carpet" greeting. Africans have a grand sense of style and treat their guests with great honor. They would not even allow me to carry my own handbag! Being from a village, it was quite an adjustment for me to receive this royalty treatment.

After a rest, the pastor asked me to teach her group of about 200 elders the "Redeeming the Land" prayer strategy. After two hours of tedious teaching, a select group piled into several vehicles and we headed for the coastal city of Badagry. Badagry, known as "The Cradle of Christianity" in Africa was also the seaport for the exchange of African slaves. Several hundred years ago, a Muslim king sold his own Nigerian people as slaves to the English and Americans. The pastor told me we would go to the port where the ships boarded the slaves that were bound for America. After redeeming the land at this site, she told me we would visit three other key points of interest.

We took the Communion elements with us, partook of the Communion and then, with the anointing oil in hand, walked and prayed over the coastal area of Badagry where the slave trade took place, breaking the powers that held the people in bondage. It was a very moving experience for me to listen to the pastor's prayer in the Yoruba language. Even though I could not understand one word, I could sense a powerful authority in the commands spoken to the demonic powers.

I struggled in my mind how a king could sell his own people as if they were animals in exchange for a small profit. When we finished the prayer strategy, we got in our cars and drove in front of a very old, two-story building. The pastor told me as we were ascending the stairs this building was the very place the first Anglican missionary painstakingly translated the Bible into the Yoruba language. It took him fourteen years to do that holy work. As we walked

105

around the building, we could hear the creaking of old boards and sensed the lingering presence of the Lord.

When we finished the tour, we drove to another building much smaller than the Anglican's residence. I noticed the elders seemed disturbed, but they were speaking in their language so I did not know the reason for their troubled looks. Just as we were entering the building, I asked loudly so I could be heard over their strained voices, "What is this building?" The pastor looked at me and said, "This is the building where they house the slaves' chains." When I entered the room this horrific grief hit my spirit, and I screamed out in pain, covering my mouth trying to muffle my loud cries and groans.

They introduced me to a boy about eleven or twelve years of age and told me he was the great, great, great, great grandson of the king who sold his people into slavery! The pastor paid the boy so I could take photos. He pointed to the leg and hand chains so my assistant could snap the picture. Then he put a rectangular piece of rusted iron implement around his mouth showing me where it goes. With his index finger, he pointed down the middle of his lips, depicting the inserted nail to keep the slaves from communicating with each other. I could hardly contain my sobs as this overwhelming grief flooded my soul of the untold suffering represented in the chains. Then he took us to a corner of the room to show us the large copper soup kettle. He bent over at his waist, revealing how the slaves stooped to put their tongues through the instrument around their lips as they slurped what little watery soup they could ingest.

I was the last one to leave, so I motioned to the young man and asked him through sign language if I could pray for him, and he nodded yes. I indicated to him to kneel and I prayed over him, asking the Lord when he grew up to use him as an evangelist to bring the Gospel of Jesus to his people. Then I spoke a prophetic word over him and left that place with mixed feelings.

Chains and Copper Kettle in House of Chains, Badagry, Nigeria, known as "The Cradle of Christianity."

The King's Palace

We finally arrived at the Muslim king's palace and were escorted to a waiting room where the entire circular wall depicted the story of the slave trade. As we were studying the narration in word pictures, an assistant greeted us and asked us to follow him. They spoke in Yoruba, so I just followed what the elders did. As each elder and the pastor walked into the inner chamber, they fell on their face, bowing before the king. I watched as they prostrated themselves, but I did not feel I needed to fall on the floor to show him honor, so I nodded my head in great respect.

The king sat upon a literal throne with two Moslem wives sitting on their thrones; one on each side of him. They had a lengthy exchange, but I did not have a clue what they were discussing. Then the king looked in my direction and spoke to me. The interpreter said to me, "The king wants to know what you thought when you saw the house of chains."

Not forewarned that the king would even speak to me, I had no prepared words for royalty, so I breathed a quick prayer before I opened my mouth to reply. As I spoke to him, my voice started to crack and my eyes reddened with restrained tears. I said something to the effect, "Sir, I am from America, the land from where we purchased your precious people as our slaves. I represent my people of America, and I want to tell you how truly sorry I am for what we have done to your people in the past. I ask for your forgiveness for this atrocity, and I pray that our nations will work together in harmony from this day forward." He starred at me for a long moment and then dismissed us after speaking to the pastor.

Riding in silence in the vehicle for as long as I could stand it, I turned to the pastor and asked her, "Please tell me what he said to you." She looked at me with a growing smile and said in almost disbelief, "He thanked us for coming and then told me I could have any piece of property in Badagry to build a Christian church!"

"I Am About to Pour Out My Spirit on Native Americans"

When I completed my ministry in Lagos, I flew to Enugu, a northern city in Nigeria to minister at my apostolic father's church, Victory Cathedral. After arriving, I told my spiritual father, Archbishop Onigbo, that I had some exciting news to share with him. In respectful silence, he listened to my testimony of our visit to the Muslim king's palace and as I was speaking, his smile slowly faded. When I finished with the testimony, he told me in his strong deep African voice, "Sista Flo, you do not know this, but recently I went to America and spoke in the largest African American church in Atlanta, Georgia. Sister Flo, what you did before the Muslim king in Badagry, I did also before my people in Atlanta, Georgia. I asked my Nigerians to forgive *us* for what we did to them by selling them into slavery to the Americans." When he finished, we were both rejoicing with tears of great joy.

I said something like this, "Don't you see what the Lord has done Brother Victor? There was transference of forgiveness in the heavenly realm across our nations, and we will see what great effect will come of this for surely our God has heard of this spiritual exchange that just happened."

Immediately after the repentance and forgiveness of both races, I noticed more and more black ministers on Christian television and many articles of up-and-coming black evangelists in the Christian magazines. A powerful revival was breaking forth in every camp among believers of the black race and it was exciting to watch! The mighty God in Heaven saw every tear they cried, felt every pain they had in their tortured bodies, and it was now time for great restitution—revival in the land!

As I rejoiced watching the grand display of God's power among my precious black brothers and sisters, the Holy Spirit spoke to me and said, "What I did for the blacks in the past thirty years, I am about to do for your people!" Hallelujah!

Chapter 9

MIGHTY WARRIORS CONFERENCE

I turned on Christian television and there he was again, telling about the exciting signs, wonders, and miracles that were occurring in his ministry on the East Coast. I hollered to Mike, "Honey, come here. Listen to this man from South Africa. He's telling about a great move of God that has broken out here in America." Mike asked his name and I said, "Rodney Howard-Browne." Mike listened for a few more minutes but he had to leave to finish a project, but I stayed glued to the TV as the South African finished his testimony. While I was listening to him, the Holy Spirit said to me, "Call TBN and ask for his phone number and invite him to minister in Juneau." I called TBN, and got his office number. I quickly dialed but only got his voicemail, so I left a message, inviting him to come to Juneau.

The next day I asked Mike if he called, and to my great disappointment, Mike said, "No." However, the following day the phone rang and I jumped up, grabbed it, and answered. A deep male's voice with a thick South African accent inquired, "Is this Flo Ellers?"

"Yes," I replied. He said he was Rodney Howard-Browne and I exclaimed, "You're kidding?"

He replied, "Well, you called me didn't you?"

I said, "Well, yes. I call everyone, but they never call me back!" In the course of our conversation, he agreed to come to Juneau for a week to minister revival meetings. I was outrageously joyful and could hardly contain myself. I had to find Mike to share the good news with him. After I told him, he asked me where I would get the money to rent the public venue for the week of meetings. I told him the money would come in when the revival broke out, but for the first time, he opposed my plan and told me to ask my pastor to host the meetings.

Reluctantly, I made the appointment with my pastor, Mike Rose of Juneau Christian Center, and told him all about Rodney's revival meetings. "Pastor Mike, we have three choices:

1. You can let me use the church facility without charge;

2. We can do the meetings together;

3. You can take the meetings."

He did not even blink or bow his head in prayer but said, "I'll take the meetings!" I thought to myself,

No Pastor Mike, that is not the right answer! At the time, I did not know the Lord was dealing with Pastor Rose about a coming move of God in our church and said to him, "I will take you from survival to revival!"

Evangelist Rodney came with his beautiful wife, Adonica. During the first few days, revival broke out in Juneau! He planned to stay one week, but the meetings extended to three weeks. At the end of the first week, I got on the phone (I was the town crier) and called everyone I knew from my village of Klawock in the south—all the way up to Anchorage! The news spread rapidly as spiritually hungry people began flying in from all over the state, some from as far away as Pt. Barrow! Joy was in the camp, many were saved and delivered; terminal diseases were healed; and even a lame woman walked out of her wheelchair! All of those who were touched in those meetings went forth from there delivered from worldly desires to heavenly fires.

Mighty Warriors Conference

A year or so after that Alaskan revival, the Lord spoke to me and told me to have a "Mighty Warriors Conference" (MWC) inviting all the key Native American leaders to Oklahoma for a week of meetings. The Holy Spirit had shown me a map of the United States, highlighting the state of Oklahoma. I noticed how Oklahoma, shaped like a door key, would be a "key" in unlocking revival for our nation! My good friend, Mike Choate (now gone to heaven), also had a

113

vision of Oklahoma. He saw three flames coming up out of the middle of the U.S. and as they grew in size, they began to twirl around each other and became one mighty flame of revival.

Again, I contacted Rodney Howard-Browne and invited him to Oklahoma for the Mighty Warriors Conference, and he agreed to come for five nights. Leaders from Alaska, Washington State, Oregon, Canada, and many cities in Oklahoma descended upon the Pentecostal campground just outside of Oklahoma City. They came with great expectation for an outpouring from on high, and they were not disappointed! From the first night, the power of God came blowing into the meetings as the evangelist spoke about the anointing of God. Signs, wonders, and miracles occurred nightly. Lives were dramatically changed as the Lord touched His people. Several had a spiritual encounter like Saul on the road to Damascus (see Acts 9). In all the revival meetings I have been to around the world, that week in Oklahoma was among the most glorious I have ever experienced.

You Have Breast Cancer!

Two months before my scheduled Mighty Warriors Conference, my doctor diagnosed me with breast cancer. After the lumpectomy, he strongly suggested I fly to Seattle for six weeks of radiation and chemotherapy. My husband concurred and we made plans to leave immediately. Mike and I took a small apartment a couple of blocks from the Seattle cancer institute, and I started my treatments. The doctor told me I would become weak from the combination of chemo and radiation, but I had no adverse reactions. In fact, I felt just fine. My very good friend, Pastor Les Moore, from Oregon brought a couple of his elders from his church to visit me and they commented how well I looked. They said, "You do not look like you have had a sick day in your life." I think they came to pray for me but went home rejoicing in my well-being.

On the last Friday of my six-week treatments, the doctor told me he had miscalculated the number of treatments and instead of Friday being the last treatment, he said I needed to return the following week for two more. I told him it was impossible because I was flying out on Saturday (the following day) to Oklahoma. After much haggling with the doctor, we agreed I would receive all three treatments in one day. He warned me that much radiation would deplete all my strength, but I told him to okay it with the lab.

Later that morning, I walked to the cancer lab and had all three treatments. As the technician was lowering the table I was lying on, I swung my legs over the side and jumped off. He tried to stop me, thinking I was going to fall, but I stood upright, looked at him, raised my hand in the air, and yelled out in a loud voice, "Hall-le-lu-jah!"

Then he said to me with this startled look on his face, "Mrs. Ellers, I hope I never see you in here again!" He gave me a big smile and I walked out the door.

115

Overwhelmed by Kindness

At the beginning of that sixth week of treatment, I received a phone call from my best friend, Reverend Sheila Marks from Pennsylvania. She told me her husband was paying for her hotel and her airfare to Seattle so she could come to intercede for me before I left for my Oklahoma conference. I was speechless! I have never had anyone do such a kind deed for me, and she was not getting a thing in return. I could not fathom this depth of God's love for me.

My Hair Grows Back!

Because of the combination of the oral and IV chemo drugs coupled with six weeks of radiation, of course I started to lose my hair by the handfuls. I could see my scalp and I knew in a couple of days that I would be bald! However, I never gave it a second thought. I do not know why . . . I guess I was just too excited to get to the Mighty Warriors Conference. I mentioned my hair loss to Sheila and she and her prayer warriors started interceding for the restoration of my hair. She stood on the Scripture from Luke 21:18 where Jesus said, "But not a hair of your head shall be lost." When I boarded my Saturday flight to Oklahoma, all my hair had grown back supernaturally! Glory to God!

Thereafter, when Mike and I would go to the large shopping malls and were separated, he said he would just look down the long halls at the shoppers and spot me immediately. I asked him how he knew it was me, and he said there was *something unusual* about my hair. I told him it is because my hair came from Heaven; it is "glory" hair!

Dr. Negiel Bigpond, Morning Star Church of All Nations

Dancing in the Glory

In the opening night of the conference, Pastor Negiel Bigpond started playing the keyboard as only he can and the anointing hit the place. Everyone got up and started dancing before the Lord. There was a liberty in the Lord rarely experienced in church. The people uninhibited whooped and shouted before the Lord as all their cares fell away. I danced before the Lord night after night with great enthusiasm. The doctors told me I would be so weak, but the Lord showed *His* might in and through me.

It was during the fourth night of the Oklahoma gathering while Rodney was preaching from Acts 12:24, "But the Word of God grew and multiplied" that the anointing of God's touch came upon me in a very powerful way. He quoted that scripture repeatedly as I was sliding out of my seat! I silently prayed, "Not now Lord, not while Brother Rodney is preaching!" but the Holy Spirit continued His work. All of a sudden, it felt like I could not breathe. I was trying desperately to inhale, but I could not seem to get any air. A brother sitting directly behind me thought I was in serious trouble, so he got out of his seat to assist me when Rodney said to him, "Leave her alone, brother. She will be all right."

I thought, *Yeah that is easy for you to say. You are not the one trying to get a breath*. Then, as suddenly as it began, it stopped. I inhaled deeply and regained my dignity sitting upright in my chair. Immediately after the meeting, three prophets came to me and each said the same thing. They said they saw a hand cover my face and then watched me struggling for a breath. As they were watching this takes place, a second hand — a much larger hand — grabbed the hand covering my face and pulled it away. When that happened, they said I took a deep breath and sat up.

I believe what they saw was this: The first hand was the spirit of cancer, the spirit of death smothering me; and the second hand that peeled it back was the hand of the Lord and I was healed from cancer. From that night, I have claimed the Scripture in Nahum 1:9, "What do you conspire against the Lord? He will make an utter end of it. Affliction will not rise up the second time." The cancer never came back and I have been cancer free since 1991.

$7,000 for 7000 Souls

On the fifth day of the Mighty Warriors Conference, Brother Rodney came to me and spoke with me privately and told me he had to leave the meetings to go home. He said my people needed to hear me preach the last night. I stopped him and said, "No! You cannot leave. You agreed to stay five nights." However, I gave up after seeing I could not persuade him to continue with the revival meetings.

Then he asked me, "How much money was taken in?" I told him exactly $7,000.

He said, "I want you to keep that money and use it for your people."

I again protested, saying it is your money, you earned it. He again replied, but this time with tears in his eyes, "No Flo, I want you to keep that money and use it for your people."

I was deeply moved by the graciousness of this man of God from South Africa. I said to him, "You know, Brother Rodney, I asked many big name evangelists to come and minister but because we are 'just a bunch of Indians,' they would not come . . . but *you* came; and because you came and ministered to the Native Americans, I believe the Lord will give you that nationwide revival you have greatly longed for."

Worldwide Revival Breaks Out!

That following week, Rodney Howard-Browne walked into a church in Lakeland, Florida, (just four days after the Oklahoma MWC) and a mighty move of God broke out in Lakeland, which lasted initially three weeks. There were 7,000 people gloriously saved! To Jesus is all the glory for the 7,000 souls for the $7,000. Hallelujah.

The pastor of the church and Brother Rodney took a week off to rest and resumed the meetings for several more weeks. During one of the glorious meetings at the Lakeland Church, a young discouraged evangelist was mightily touched. He left that Lakeland revival and flew to Toronto, carrying the same heavenly fire into those meetings! What broke out in Canada was called the "Father's Blessing" or the "Toronto Blessing," which then spread worldwide.

Thousands more had an encounter with the Lord Jesus Christ and took the anointing of power to many nations of the world . . . and it all started with a missionary from South Africa touching the host people of America—the Native Americans with the eternal flame of revival!

Chapter 10

GOD'S REVIVALISTS OF GLORY!

Sitting across the round table from me was our stalky Israeli tour guide. As he opened his mouth wide and spooned down the thick golden olive oil, followed by the typical Mediterranean breakfast, he smiled and reminded us how healthy olive oil was for the body. Our discussion turned from polite conversation to the present tensions in the Middle East. As he shared with us about their land, the discussion flowed to the military. He told us when he was a young man, he was part of the elite combat fighting team called the "Haganah." This highly trained security force helped Israel become a nation in 1948.

I was intrigued to hear about this band of soldiers and I wanted to hear more. I told him, to his surprise, that I, too, was a Haganah and had recently been in my village of Klawock to visit my family and to conduct revival meetings on our island. When my uncle came to pick me up in his new red truck, he had placed the hyphenated word *Ha-ga-nah* on the front bumper. I asked him what that Tlingit word meant and he said a loose translation was, "When the going gets tough, the tough get going."

I told our Israeli guide our Haganah is spelled exactly the way the Jews spell their elite fighting force; and our warriors were the same as the Israelis. He stood up, reached out his hand across the table, clasped my hand with a firm grip and said, "From one Haganah to another Haganah." We smiled in affirmation of one another and left for a day's touring in the land of the Bible.

Our DNA

Our spiritual DNA of the Haganah is to be warriors with a servant's heart of love. However, our battles do not include flesh and blood. We wrestle against spiritual forces in heavenly places. We do not fight with one another but against Satan's hosts of demons binding the people who belong to God. In dealing with fragile humanity, we must be a servant of love, mercy, and kindness. Jesus said in Mark 10:44 (KJV), "And whosoever of you will be the *chiefest*, shall be the servant of all" (My emphasis).

Put on Your Armor

In Ephesians 6, the apostle Paul teaches us to put on (and we should never take off) our armor as the Roman's armor that covered the entire body. The only place not protected is the soldier's back. Each soldier knew the one on his right and the one on his left, so he would have added help when engaged in a battle too strong for him. It is the same in the army of God. However, occasionally, the one who is supposed to watch your back ends up being the one who wounds your back. I have been in full time ministry for many years and I have encountered many battles, but no battle hurts more than the wounds inflicted by friends. As I have watched others, I find this has also been true in their life or ministry as well. I believe the Lord could have stopped *that* battle, but He allowed it and used it to develop godly character in each one of us.

For me, the spirit of rejection has been the most difficult to deal with. As a Native American, the whites looked down on me as someone who had less value than them. Only a recipient of racism can be the judge of the depth of its hatred and the accompanying pain.

How Do You See Yourself?

As a woman minister, some of my male counterparts treated me with great disrespect. The Amish are not the only ones to practice shunning. If my cousin Evangelist Glenn Anniskette had not given me a prophetic word from the Lord about this spirit of rejection in the early days of my ministry, I am sure I would have quit the ministry a long time ago. The Lord, in His great wisdom, knows what we will go through and He prepares us for every battle. He alone helps us conquer the regrets in life and brings us into His victory! The key to getting past the fight to the victory side is to never see yourself as a victim. I do not believe in victimization theology, but I believe in the victory of the Cross. I appropriate Jesus' victorious reign and refuse to feel sorry for myself. We are "taller" because we are using the stones of adversity as stepping-stones. God will deal with the injustice; but we must deal with our lack of love and forgiveness.

In the Old Testament, the ten spies who went into the Promise Land came back with a negative report of what they thought were insurmountable obstacles—including the giants in the land. They told their leader, Moses, the giants saw them as "grasshoppers." They came into agreement with the giants and saw themselves as grasshoppers. How we see ourselves is important.

I have heard that there are 7,000 promises in the Bible, and at best, we are living in about 1,000 of them. I do not know about you, but I am tired of sitting in the back of the bus. My God has shown us a land of promise, full of milk and honey and all that we will ever need in this life. Yes, there are giants in the land, but I have had it with the giants. They have been sucking on my grapes long enough! My attitude is radical. I am going into my land, rip off the giants' lips, and take back from them what they have no right to inherit!

The Cherokee Cry

During WW II, the motto in the 101st Airborne was *Currahee!* which is the Cherokee cry that means "We

Stand Alone Together." It was also the motto of the Episcopal Academy Novice Crew Team who were known to scream *Currahee!* when in the final stretch of a race!

We, as the Body of Christ are in the final stretch of our race. At the end of this age, we know the battle is going to become intense, and only the strongest will stand. Nevertheless, the other side of that battle will be the greatest outpouring of God's Spirit the world has ever witnessed—both battles will be with great intensity. Therefore, it behooves us to stand together, strengthening our resolve for the last days. All our petty differences and competition must be laid aside, striving for what matters most to God—the lost and dying.

Indian Regalia and Feathers

Finally, the days are gone of workshops that debated whether to wear feathers or not to wear feathers. I do not need to wear feathers and Indian regalia to prove I am an Indian. I was born an Indian, now I am born-again. Nevertheless, still others question whether syncretism—the blending of Christianity and culture—is allowed in our churches. I do not know the complete answer to that question; I can only rely upon the wisdom of God to guide us. We have 500 tribes and each people group has their own distinct customs and traditions. Each must seek the Lord to find out what is allowable and what is not. For me, syncretism is another form of bondage in the guise of deception. It is not "Jesus *and* anything." It is "Jesus only," and I am not talking about a denomination.

There are many beautiful customs and traditions in the native culture, and I choose to emphasize those. I want to see a renewal of the part of our culture that speaks softly to our children and that teaches our sons and daughters to have respect for their elders. I want to see parents teach their youth how to be self-sustaining once again and to lovingly care for each tribal member. I want to see purity and dignity restored to our people instead of shame of being a Native.

Dancing in the Fire

One integral part of being an Indian is our love of dancing. If you take the dance away from the Natives, you will take away their victory. As long as our dance is unto the Creator, or tells the story of a hunt, I say, "Let them dance." I like what an Apache pastor once said, "I used to dance around the fire, now I dance in the fire!"

More than ever, we need this heavenly fire of God in our lives and in our churches. *Fire* is the holiness of God, which consumes all that is inconsistent with Him and contrary to His Word. We need to dance in *that* fire until everything that is not of God burns off us. When the holy fire completes its work in us, God's fiery passion will consume us for people who are on their way to a hell, where *that* fire never quenches and torment never ends (see Revelation 20:14-15).

In the late '80s, the Lord Jesus spoke through a Cherokee prophet of God from Tulsa saying in part, "He [Jesus] would remove the Native American's war paint and regalia, and through the Holy Spirit, do a quick work of sanctification in them to bring them up speedily with the rest of the Body of Christ! When He completes His work, He will set them aside for His holy purpose as end-time revivalists to help usher in the last-days outpouring of God in America! Hallelujah!"

This Generation Is Searching

In the introduction of this book, I told of the native hunter whose searching led him to the desire of his longing heart. When he found the One he was looking for, he said, "I feel Your presence, but I do not know Your name."

However, what this hunter did not realize was, as he was seeking the God of heaven, the God of heaven was also seeking him! In John 6:44, Jesus said, "No man can come to me, except the Father which hath sent me draws him" (KJV).

God Looks from Heaven

The Psalmist said in Chapter 33:13-15, "The Lord looks from heaven; He sees all the sons of men. From the place of His dwelling, He looks on all the inhabitants of the earth. He fashions their hearts individually; He considers all their works."

Do you realize He is looking at you right now?

Just as God created man with eyes and ears, He has eyes and ears. He is not a ghost-like being floating around in the forest or hovering in buildings, but He

127

is a Spirit. He is the King of the universe, sitting upon a throne, looking at the sons of men, aware of their every deed and every thought. He is so massive, the earth is only His footstool. When He spoke in Genesis 1:3, "Let there be light . . ." that light continues to this day traveling at 186,000 feet per second out into the universe until God commands that light to stop.

His eyes see you and His ears are attuned to your cry. He told the Psalmist in 34:15, "The eyes of the Lord are on the righteous, and His ears are open unto their cry."

Blind Bart

Bartimaeus could hear a crowd coming, so he grabbed his can to beg for a few coins. He was hot, thirsty, and tired of sitting on the filthy ground begging. He inquired of a passerby what all the excitement was about. They told him Jesus was coming his way. Jesus, oh, I have heard of Him. Isn't He is the One who heals the sick and raises the dead? Is He coming my way? Bartimaeus cried out, "Jesus, thou Son of David, have mercy on me." Several in the crowd told him to be quiet but he yelled even louder, "Son of David, have mercy on me. So Jesus stood still. . . ." (see Mark 10:46-52 KJV).

It is difficult for me to grasp such a lofty thought: "And Jesus stood still." I cannot understand this kind of love that the God of this universe would stand still at the cry of one human being. First John 3:8 says, "For this purpose the Son of God was manifested, that he might destroy the works of the devil."

Jesus called for Bartimaeus to come to Him. When Bartimaeus heard that, he threw away his tattered garment and came to Jesus (see Mark 10:49-50). Some have said the blind wore a special covering identifying their debility, but I do not know for sure. I think the tattered garment represented his past. He knew if he could get to Jesus, everything would change in his life. He was not going to miss this opportunity, so he threw off the cloak, stood upright, and came to Jesus. When he stood in front of Jesus, he could not see Jesus, because he was blind, but Jesus could see him. Jesus asked him what he wanted. If I were Blind Bart and Jesus asked me, I might have thought, *Can't you see I am blind*? No, Jesus wanted him to articulate exactly what he wanted. The Bible says, "You have not because you ask not" (James 4:2 MKJV). Did he want a couple of coins for a meal, money to pay his rent, or perhaps money to buy new clothes? When Jesus asked him, "What do you want Me to do for you?" Bartimaeus did not hesitate. He replied, "I want my sight restored. Jesus said unto him, "Go thy way; your faith has made you well" (see Mark 48:51-52).

The Work of Satan

The Gospel of Luke 13:10-13 describes a miracle of Jesus, and I paraphrase: One Sabbath day as Jesus was teaching in the synagogue, He looked up and in walked a woman bent over double. The spiritual need in this woman's life had long surpassed the shame of her disability; she came to worship God. She hobbled to find an empty place when Jesus called out to her to come to Him. With all eyes on her, she struggled to walk upright but I am sure the severe back pain prevented her. For eighteen long, lonely years, all she saw was the filth on the ground. The only way she could embrace a loved one was when she was lying down. Night after night, she must have moaned in pain trying to get comfortable. Who is calling me, she must have thought. She shuffled up to the front and Jesus said to her as she strained to twist her neck to look at Him. "Woman, you are loosed from your infirmity" (Luke 13:12), He said in a firm voice. Then He laid His hands on her and she stood upright for the first time in eighteen years and glorified God!

When she came into that synagogue that day, she could not see Him, but He could see her. He saw her need and heard her silent plea for freedom from her awful shame and horrible pain. Acts 10:38 says of Jesus: "How God anointed Jesus of Nazareth with the Holy Ghost and with power; who went about doing good, and healing all that were oppressed of the devil; for God was with Him" (KJV).

Stand Up Warrior-son; Stand Erect Warrior-daughter!

The Bible says in Luke 13:16 that Satan was the one who inflicted this precious woman with that deforming disease. God sent His only begotten Son from heaven to set humanity free from the bondages of Satan (see John 3:16). God did not create man to sit in the dirt and grovel on the ground like blind Bart or to have her body twisted in pain like the woman in the synagogue. No, God created us to stand erect and to stand with dignity as *Chief Walkin' Tall*.

Just as the Lord used a one-eyed black man in the Azusa Street outpouring at the beginning of the twentieth century, He is going to use another despised race—the Native Americans—in the coming revival. The Lord said the Gospel of His Kingdom would be preached to all the world—to every ethnic group—and then the end would come. The Native Americans are one of the last ethnic groups to receive the Pentecostal experience. When they embrace the sacred fire from heaven, they will go like "firebrands" throughout this nation to help usher in the end-time move of God to the Americas.

The Tsunami of God's Power Is Here!

Many years ago, the Lord showed me in a night vision the coming of an unprecedented move of God that will bring tremendous power to set the captives free and power to heal twisted, broken humanity. There are those who have gone to many to set them free of the most despicable bondages, but the power was not there to set them completely free. However, in this last move of God *everything* will be possible!

When my vision ended, I could scarcely breathe because my room was flooded with the fiery presence of God. What He showed was so overwhelming, my carnal mind could not contain it. The vision caused me to be in awe as the reverential fear of the Lord filled my heart.

When I shared the vision, some said it has already come and gone, but I do not think *what* I saw has past, but it is just *now* beginning to break forth upon the church of America. Those who have prepared themselves and totally surrendered to the Holy Spirit will be a part of this move of God. I believe the Native Americans will be a major part of this outpouring. They are going to be last day's revivalists carrying the harvester's anointing of power and glory to set the captives free! The world is about to see the greatest demonstration of God's power they have ever witnessed. What is coming will make the Day of Pentecost look like a Sunday school picnic. The culmination of God's outpouring will be as if He had taken all previous moves for the past 2,000 years of Church history, roll it together as one, and then pour it upon humanity. That is what I see coming!

The Vision

I was standing over a vast ocean when I noticed it beginning to rise. It started as a ground swell. As I watched, the vast expanse of the water rose higher and higher. I felt a fear and began to back away when, suddenly, the ground swell became a tidal wave. As it loomed up before me, I watched this monstrous wave beginning to crest, and then it was coming toward me at tremendous speed. I tried to outrun it, because I knew if this wave crashed over me, it would destroy me. I could not outrun it. As I looked up into the deep blue wave, it descended down upon me. Instead of crushing me, it came up under me, lifted me up and whooshed me into the most glorious heavenly land I have ever seen.

How a Tsunami Begins

A tsunami, or tidal wave, begins deep at the ocean floor. My understanding is that two tectonic plates under the ocean rub together, causing an earthquake. One way to detect this underwater disturbance is to view the ripples on top of the water. Before the tsunami forms, the ocean pulls back the water from the beach as if some invisible force is sucking it out. There is an eerie silence for a few moments, and then comes this loud crescendo as the tsunami comes rushing toward the beach at 500 miles per hour, moving everything out of its way. When you see the tsunami loom up before you, it is too late to run for cover.

It Is Time for Us to Change History!

I believe the interpretation is this: We are now in the last days of this *age* and time—as we understand time—will soon end. Those who are near to the heart of God have felt the shaking and sense the end-time move of God has begun in the deeps of their heart . . . for they are men and women of great faith. They know when this tsunami comes, it will be *the* wave that will end all waves. They look at the ocean's covering and see a ripple here and a ripple there, but they know "This ain't it!" They are not part of the company who is standing uselessly on the seashore waiting for the coming of the Lord. That company of believers watched as the tide was sucked out, the water was gone, and thought the end was near. However, the Lord has another company of believers—the Ha-ga-nah, the Joshuas, and the Calebs of this generation who know by the Spirit what is seen with the natural eye is not the way it shall be. They know by the hearing of the ear something big is coming, and the Day of Pentecost will pale in comparison to it.

Expectantly, the tidal wave they have waited for so long is now here! It is looming on the distant horizon, and men's hearts are starting to quake before a holy God who is coming with power and great glory! The ground is shaking at the crescendo of the roar as the tsunami is rushing toward the shores of America!

EPILOGUE

The anatomy or analysis of a biblical revival is noteworthy for those who are preparing for the coming move of God particularly in North America. In my study on an outpouring I have noted there are seven *"greats"* in the Book of Acts revival and they are:

- Acts 4:33, *And with **great power** gave the apostles witness of the resurrection of the Lord Jesus: and **great grace** was upon them all.*

With every awakening, every renewal or revival there is always great power and great grace poured out upon the people. However, this is where we must be very careful because heaven is especially near during an outpouring. Acts chapter five recounts the story of a couple named Ananias and Sapphira who promised to donate the proceeds of the sale of their property to the work of God. However, they were deceptive about it and retained a portion of the money. They refused to pay the price of revival, which is honesty, integrity and genuineness. They lied to Peter, but the apostle prophetically revealed to them that in reality, they had lied to God. When they heard Peter's words, they fell down dead. Here is the biblical account:

- Acts 5: 5, 11, *And Ananias hearing these words fell down, and gave up the ghost: and **great fear** came on all them that heard these things . . . And **great fear** came upon all the church, and upon as many as heard these things.*

In the past few years, the church has heard a constant message of "grace, grace, grace" until the church has become a disgrace! It is time for the fear of the Lord to grip our congregations again. When the church is awestruck by the Presence of the Lord in our services, we will put down our lattes and muffins, pick up our Bibles, cover our cleavage, turn off the smoke machines and cry out for the lost and dying. When the fear of the Lord returns and we cry out in repentance, great power will return once again to a lack luster church.

- Acts 6:8, *And Stephen, full of faith and power, did **great wonders and miracles** among the people.*

However, not everyone will be excited your church is having a revival. When the Holy Spirit begins to release His powerful anointing and people are set free from bondages, financial ruin and diseases, our ancient enemy, the devil, will rage against what God is doing. Remember when Simeon prophesied and blessed Joseph and Mary, declaring over the eight-day-old Messiah, *"Behold, this child is set for the fall and rising again of many in Israel; and for a sign which shall be spoken against"* (Luke 2:34). When Jesus grew up into manhood and the anointing of God rested upon Him, Satan began an assault against Him, and he will do the same to you. You will also be a *"sign which shall be spoken against."*

- Acts 8:1, *And Saul was consenting unto his death. And at that time there was a* **great persecution** *against the church which was at Jerusalem; and they were all scattered abroad throughout the regions of Judea and Samaria, except the apostles.*

Saul was a religious fanatic thinking he was doing God's will when he consented to have Stephen stoned with rocks. Stephen was the church's first martyr. As the church began, so shall it be at its end. Whatever is at the beginning of any move will ultimately be at its conclusion. As they were pelting him with rocks, Stephen cried out for forgiveness, and the heavens opened!

- Acts 8:2, *And devout men carried Stephen to his burial, and made* **great lamentation** *over him.*

As Saul continued relentlessly, the persecution had a counter-effect, fueling the flames of revival. Because of the persecution, the apostles and the early evangelists finally began to fulfill the Great Commission, traveling to regions beyond where the Gospel had never been preached and multitudes were saved. Their mourning over Stephen turned into Holy Spirit joy.

- Acts 8:3-8, *As for Saul, he made havoc of the church, entering into every house, and hailing men and women committed them to prison. Therefore, they that were scattered abroad went everywhere preaching the word. Then Philip went down to the city of Samaria, and preached Christ unto them. And the people with one accord gave heed unto those things which Philip spoke, hearing and seeing the miracles which he did. For unclean spirits, crying with loud voice, came out of many that were possessed with them; and many taken with palsies, and that were lame, were healed. And there was* **great joy** *in that city.*

So we see that the signs of a heaven-sent awakening or revival are: great power, great grace, great fear, great wonders and miracles, great persecution, great lamentation and great joy.

When you participate in a heaven-on-earth visitation like this, the following fruit will be evidenced in your life:

1. You will fall in love with Jesus all over again;
2. You will experience supernatural love for the lost;
3. Prayer meetings will be jammed;
4. There will be increased missionary zeal;
5. Many souls will be swept into the Kingdom of God.

There is a divine timing in any move of God. *"And when the day of Pentecost was fully come…"*

What do you think will precipitate the coming awakening or the promised revival? Will it be fasting and prayer, or repentance, or judgment, or maybe all three?

The Holy Spirit has been preparing a host of last day's harvesters with a harvester's anointing. Many are young with fresh zeal, but many others are men and women of old age who thought their day had come and gone. The Lord has been speaking to them saying, "Don't give up on your dream ... for what I spoke to you in days gone by will come to pass, for the time appointed to fulfill the vision is here. The Scripture even says, *"Your old men shall dream dreams..."* (Acts 2:17).

Another radical group of revivalists are about to be released. They have been in the Word and prayer seeking the Lord for His plan for the ages. They are like Paul, the apostle; they are not afraid of suffering for the Gospel or for Jesus' sake.

> But the Lord said unto him, "Go thy way; for he is a chosen vessel unto Me, to bear My name before the Gentiles, and kings, and the children of Israel: for I will show him how **great things** he must suffer for My name's sake" (Acts 9:15-16).

All those willing to walk in Paul's footsteps have been prepared for this day; they are not afraid to suffer greatly. They live for Jesus alone . . . and in so doing, each of them qualifies to be a *Chief Walkin' Tall*.